Notorious Pittsburgh

Christopher Whitlatch

With illustrations by Joe Wos

DEDICATION

Notorious Pittsburgh is dedicated to the wonderful true crime fans that joined me for the walking tours and brought these stories to life. Thank you!

Forward

I'm Christopher Whitlatch, and for the past few years I have hosted two walking tours in downtown Pittsburgh. Both tours share stories of Pittsburgh's more notorious past. The first tour I created was of Pittsburgh's former red-light district along Penn and Liberty Avenues.

That tour came about by accident. I was working for the Pittsburgh Foundation, a philanthropic organization serving the region, at the time of the Pittsburgh Cultural Trust's 25th anniversary. The CEO of the Foundation then was Grant Oliphant.

He came to me and said, "Chris, you are good at finding things online, find me some photos of what these buildings look liked before the Cultural Trust acquired them." Many of the former red-light locations are now cultural locations, and several others were torn down to make for other public amenities.

When I began researching, I turned to Google Archives and pulled up newspaper story after newspaper story. They read like the script to Goodfellas. I started taking copious notes and went down several rabbit holes.

What emerged was a picture of the city from the late sixties to the early eighties. There were murders, explosions and larger than life characters like Tex Gill. I put the places and people together and walked it for the first time, I decided to make it a tour.

By another chance meeting, I interviewed Bonnie Baxter for a show I do on Pittsburgh Community Television (PCTV) called Into Pittsburgh. Bonnie founded and is the executive director of Doors Open Pittsburgh. The organization hosts a yearly weekend event in October that celebrates the architecture of Pittsburgh by opening the buildings for special access.

Docents are positioned at each building to educate guests about the history and present of the space. I told Bonnie about my red-light stories and volunteered to be a docent if one of the buildings I had a story for was part of the event. She asked me how many stories I had. I said, "I have a whole tour." Bonnie had launched a new program as part of the event called Insider Tours. She invited me to bring the Red-Light Tour to the program.

The second tour was more planned. I wanted to see if I could put together enough stories to do a loop on the other side of downtown. I began researching and found there were many great and notorious stories for this loop. Thus, the Notorious Pittsburgh Tour was launched and became part of the Doors Open Pittsburgh event.

It also gave the name to this book. I've included the stories from both tours in the pages that follow, along with a few of my other favorites from outside of downtown. The last story in this book does not take place in the past. I took some liberty to include a look at what might or might not be a potential future notorious story for Pittsburgh. You can be the judge.

If all these mentions of Doors Open Pittsburgh have piqued your interest, then check them out at doorsopenpgh.org.

Why tell the seedier stories of Pittsburgh?

First, I don't think you can truly appreciate where Pittsburgh is now, unless you have a picture of where it has been. Pittsburgh is good at many things. What it may be best at, is remaking itself over and over again. In fact, the city may have perfected it, having emerged from imminent ruin several times.

There is another phenomenon as well. If you run into someone from Pittsburgh somewhere else in the World, they will regale you with how great the city is. However, inside of the city, a Pittsburgher suffers from a lack of self-esteem and will often tear down their beloved city.

This juxtaposition means we often sweep things under the rug, or in Pittsburghese, we "reddup". I don't believe these stories should be lost just because they come from across the line.

I also believe that we have a natural fascination for the stories of things we would never do, but might fantasize, romanticize or are just plain curious about. Visitors to the city and residents alike have taken the tours. Young and old, they were drawn to these stories because they don't hear about them from other places.

If we are being honest, then we must admit that Pittsburgh was just built by our titans of industry. I ask everyone at the start of the tour, what built Pittsburgh? Almost every has answered that Pittsburgh was built on coal and steel. That is true, but I would argue that it was built on take home pay.

It was the workers of Pittsburgh that built the neighborhoods and were most responsible for Pittsburgh's economy. Make no mistake, the work was hard. It provided a good living and as they said, "there was a chicken in every pot because of it."

When you work that hard, you need something to take your mind off of it. There was a bar outside of every mill and factory that was often open for every shift change. You could come in dirty, sweaty, and greasy from your tough shift and have a beer and a shot to help ease some of that pain and help you get off to sleep at night.

If you wanted to play harder, well you could take an excursion downtown and spend a little more of that hard-earned pay on some other earthly delights.

As interest and profits grew for these types of activities, so did the less-than-legal businesspeople that took advantage of it. What is most interesting to me though, is that in Pittsburgh, it was not always a professional criminal. Many times, it was someone trying to get a little more. An ironworker, a firefighter or some other enterprising individual that was willing to take risks for greater rewards.

It is for them that I write this book. Their stories should be told just like the stories of Carnegie and Frick.

Appreciate how beautiful and what an amenity that the Cultural District is by knowing that X-rated theaters, bookstores and rub joints previously inhabited these spaces. Marvel at the gleaming castle of glass that is PPG Place, knowing that one of Pittsburgh's nuisance bars formerly stood there. Celebrate the achievement of the August Wilson Center that replaced what was likely the seediest block in Pittsburgh.

That is why I tell the seedy, notorious stories of Pittsburgh. I hope you find them as entertaining and fascinating as I do. I hope also that it helps you appreciate even more that Pittsburgh is a model for reinvention.

So, I guess this is a love story after all.

CONTENTS

ACKNOWLEDGMENTS

I could not have accomplished this book without the help of Melissa Carey. She liked the stories so much that she volunteered to edit this book. she made sure that what you read was readable. Because of her, I am a better writer as well as a storyteller.

The cover design was expertly created by Rachel Arnold Sager of Second Block Studios. She has helped me many of times with my professional and personal projects.

When I asked Joe Wos if he would take on the illustrations for this book, he enthusiastically said yes, despite the myriad of his other projects. He is living his dream and helped live mine as well. Thanks, Joe!

There are so many others I should thank. Thanks to my family for putting up with this and my other projects. My mom who was always my biggest champion and supporter no matter what outlandish ideas I had for my life and career. Thanks to my college roommate at NYU, Doug Slocum. He has been a constant cricket in my ear to keep writing.

Thanks to Mike Sorg for filming my tours. Thanks to Bonnie Baxter for constantly asking me if it is ready yet and for helping me promote. Thanks to everyone who I missed and who is yet to come.

I couldn't do this without you!

Get to Know a Different Downtown

Pittsburgh has been remade, then remade, then remade again. When it is a large re-do, Pittsburgh likes to call it a renaissance. There have already been three of these that have reshaped the downtown, added to the skyline, and demolished or simply overtook areas in redevelopment efforts.

This has happened in many of the neighborhoods outside of downtown as well, often at the expense of the current inhabitants. The first to sections of this book are shaped by this theme.

In the next section, the stories will be of places that are no longer there. They have been wiped from Pittsburgh's history to make way for its future.

In this first section, however, remnants remain. The building may have been repurposed, the neighborhoods may have shrunk, or, in the case of Grant Street, the landscape may have been significantly altered. If you look hard enough, and through the stories, you can still capture the essence of the place.

1 Judges, Lawyers, and Prostitutes Oh My

It all starts here at the Executive Lounge, sometimes called the Court Lounge for its location in the shadow of the Allegheny Courthouse and amongst many of the law offices and city government buildings.

Because of its location at 504 Court Place, the Executive Lounge was a popular drinking palace for judges, attorneys, politicians, and other government officials. It featured a bartender that was one of Pittsburgh's greatest storytellers as well as a talented piano player.

The servers were special as well. An advertisement in 1965 was seeking an attractive cocktail hostess willing to wear a costume.

The Executive Lounge was also home to prostitutes, organized crime members and all sorts of other criminal elements. The legitimate and illegitimate mixed and mingled, negotiated business deals, and conducted other activities.

It is fitting that this is the first story in this book because many of the people in later stories socialized at the Lounge. George Lee owned the establishment with his silent partner, Anthony Lagatutta, and many of their vice employees and their organized crime buddies worked or hung out in the bar. Sasha Scott and Sue Dixon worked the room as call girls. Richard Henkel met Dixon there and began dating her. Sasha, Sue, Richard, and others will appear later in this book, and the Executive Lounge will pop up again.

For Lee this was a legitimate business investment that he could use to hide some of his illegitimate gains. He would often meet people here and entertain, but it was Lagatutta that used the Lounge as his hangout.

Joseph DeMarco was listed as the manager of the establishment. In 1975, that would change. DeMarco was indicted in a large numbers racket business. Just one of the criminal activities that could be partaken at the Executive.

A few years later, DeMarco was dead. He was found inside a car trunk at Greater Pittsburgh International Airport. He was shot several times and the scene was described as bloody and grisly. His body was found a few days after the actual murder took place.

The Executive Lounge did not miss a beat with DeMarco's arrest. The authorities knew it well and it was subjected to Liquor Control Board (LCB) raids on a regular basis. The bar was fined several thousand dollars on each occasion for a variety of offenses, but most often serving visibly intoxicated patrons and aiding and abetting prostitution.

During one raid, a woman known only as Charlotte offered to spend the night with one of the undercover enforcement officers for $100. For $50, she would perform any other single act.

Lagattuta was popular at the bar. He would socialize with all the patrons flashing his genial smile. He did not drink though. He could play piano and was well versed in classical music. He would sit down at the Executive's piano and bang out tunes for everyone in the lounge.

Lagattuta had a sharp mind. He could solve complex math problems without pen and paper. He was also fond of William Shakespeare and would quote from his plays in normal conversation. He also was an accomplished poker player. He claimed to have learned to play from legends in Las Vegas and often made trips there.

His legend would be complete following a brush with an FBI agent. It was a chilly fall evening in Pittsburgh. Lagattuta had noticed there was a car tailing him. He stopped at a gas station and bought two coffees. He approached the agent's vehicle. The agent rolled down the window not sure what to expect.

Lagattuta handed him one of the cups of coffee through the window. With a grin, he said, "If you're going to follow me all night, you might as well stay toasty warm." Lagattuta got back in his car, and the agent was left speechless by his act of kindness.

Lagattuta did have a past. As a member of the Pittsburgh family, he ran numbers, gambling operations insurance fraud, and other rackets. He was also accomplished with a match. In 1972, he was accused of arson when he burned down a poor performing after hours club that he owned in the Beltzhoover neighborhood.

He would be convicted of wire fraud for attempting to collect $160,000 in insurance with three other men. Sentenced to a five-year federal prison term, he served about a year and a half before his release. Lagattuta went right back to the Executive Lounge.

Lagattuta tooled around Pittsburgh in a big black Cadillac Limousine despite George Lee's urging to give it up. Lee felt it drew too much attention and heat was beginning to build on their operations. Federal agents were poking around Majestic News, Lee's pornographic distribution company.

It would all start to unravel in 1976. Under suspicion for arson again, this time when the Sportsman Lounge burned on Sixth Street. The establishment was owned by Lee and Lagattuta and was losing money.

On January 10, 1976, an attorney by the name of Edward Hutton was drinking at the Executive Lounge. Lagattuta was sitting at the bar and the piano player was entertaining guests. As Hutton imbibed, he became more and more belligerent, slinging insults at several of the patrons and staff.

Witnesses said that Lagattuta was attempting to defuse the situation and calm Hutton down. Hutton reportedly began insulting Lagattuta and his family, ending with, "I'm gonna kill you with my Irish fists."

Lagattuta tackled Hutton from the bar stool that he was perched on slamming him to the ground. He then proceeded to slam his head four times into the floor. The piano player in the middle of *My Blue Heaven* stopped and joined the other gawkers. Staff pulled Lagattuta from Hutton.

Hutton was pulled up into a seated position. Lagattuta, ever the businessman, yelled for him to pay his tab, but all Hutton could do was gurgle incoherently as blood dribbled from his mouth. Realizing that Hutton needed medical care, Lagattuta ordered his chauffer to take him to the hospital.

His driver, Roger Fuetter, and another man drove while Hutton lay in the backseat unconscious. Upon depositing him at the hospital, they were questioned and reported they had found Hutton on Sixth Avenue passed out, likely from a fall.

Hutton would last 18 days in the hospital. He contracted pneumonia because of his injuries and would die from it. Fuetter's story would begin to unravel. He left Lagattuta's employment and went to work for George Lee as a massage parlor manager.

Things would get worse. Lagattuta was arrested on third degree murder charges and be thrown back in jail on a parole violation. As he was awaiting trial, Lee was gunned down in February of 1977.

With Lee dead and Lagattuta in prison, the Executive Lounge which was teetering financially already could not survive and closed its doors in March, less than a month after Lee's murder. Lagattuta, having been returned to Pittsburgh to await trial, was sitting in a jail cell just a few blocks away, powerless to avert the demise of his favorite place.

The Executive's furnishings and equipment were reused in some of Lee's other former businesses. A raid later in 1977 at the Airport Businessman's Club, a fancy name for a massage parlor and prostitution house in Moon that was a five minutes-drive from the airport, confiscated a credit card machine that was still labeled "The Executive Lounge".

During the trial, Fuetter laid out the details of Hutton's fatal beating that was corroborated by other witnesses. He testified that Lagattuta told Hutton, "If you want to die, there is no problem here." Lagattuta's defense claimed that he was attempting to break up a fight between Hutton and another patron.

Fuetter also gave details on another fire at a club owned by George Lee, the Sportsmen Club. He claimed that Lee and Lagattuta ordered him to set it. He related that he took gasoline to the top floors of the six-story building. Setting it ablaze, it blew out the windows and spread to the rest of the building.

Lagattuta, for the crimes, was sentenced to twenty years in Allenwood Federal Penitentiary. Years later, another career criminal, Donald Duffy, would admit to the arson without Lagattuta's involvement. Lagattuta would use this evidence to seek an appeal but was denied.

Lagattuta passed away in 1996 of cancer at the age of 63.

The former building which sat on the corner of Grant Street, is tucked into the small road that is trumped by the Boulevard of the Allies. A small building in its place is known well by motorists as it houses a scrolling billboard that displays the day's headlines from Trib Total Media.

2 Forbidden Love and Pittsburgh's Great Escape

Ed Biddle

A story that spread like wildfire in a week, captivating the Pittsburgh population is one that still thrills well over one hundred years later. The tale of the Biddle brothers great escape with Katherine Soffel is one that is romanticized to this day.

The story begins in 1901. Ed and Jack Biddle, brothers originally from Detroit, made their way to Pittsburgh early in the year. Along the way they picked up Walter Dorman from Cleveland to form a gang of three.

Jack Biddle

They were petty thieves and hooligans and though they kept the police force running in circles for several months, they often stole worthless jewelry and other items. Sometimes they wore masks and sometimes they didn't. It was only a matter of time before they would get caught.

The gang's crime spree began in late winter and ran into spring of 1901. By summer, they would be in jail and on trial for murder. The three would enter houses late at night or early morning. They would incapacitate their victims and take what they could get their hands on, whether it was valuable or not.

Their preferred weapons were guns and chloroform. Chloroform had come into use and ready availability in the late 1800s as a means of anesthesia. Thieves had found it effective in subduing victims and began liberally applying it in their trade.

The Biddle gang, after several robberies that employed the use of chloroform, were given the moniker of the Chloroform Gang by the newspapers. The bumbling gang did not seem to know how to distinguish chloroform from other drugs, however. During one robbery, the gang found that they were holding a medical student and his wife, a nurse. Taking advantage of this good fortune, they went to a pharmacy down the block and returned with several bottles. At gunpoint, they forced the nurse to identify the chloroform.

The gang also did not stop at robbery. When the occasion would arise, they would rape the wives or daughters of their victims, often forcing the distraught husband or father to watch the depravity.

To this point, they had not killed anyone, though several people, including an elderly woman, were beaten to inches from death. The Chloroform Gang was ahead of the Pittsburgh Police force, and they continued to rob at will. In fact, the police were suppressing the reports of rape and the public was only aware of the robberies.

At 3 a.m. on April 12, 1901, the stakes would get higher. Thomas Kahney, a grocer who lived above his store on Mt. Washington, was awoken from a sound of a struggle coming from his wife's bedroom.

Kahney entered the room to see one of the gang members attempting to place a chloroform-soaked rag over the face of his wife. The attacker, upon seeing Kahney, drew his gun and spun, firing twice as he did.

Kahney struck by two bullets, staggered towards his wife's bed. He died in her arms. The burglars fled, leaving Kahney's 13-year-old son to run screaming from the house to alert the neighbors.

Informed of the murder and with the chloroform evidence that it was the gang who had been terrorizing Allegheny County homes for the past several months, the Pittsburgh Police acted. They put their best detective on the case, Patrick "Paddy" Fitzgerald.

Fitzgerald's was a longtime partner of Charles McGovern on the force. McGovern's son, fresh from service in the Calvary in the Spanish American, known as Charley "Buck" McGovern had recently joined the force as its youngest detective. Fitzgerald had taken the young McGovern under his wing and trained him. They had become best friends and Buck would soon play a fateful part in the Biddle story.

The police caught a break in the case. A few days before, a tip had been passed to them about a couple of roomers in a boarding house, a Mr. and Mrs. Wilcox. The Wilcox's were known to be running around with a Mr. and Mrs. Edward Wright and Wright's brother, John D. Wright, who lived nearby.

This clue would have normally been overlooked or buried in police files, but as there were no other strong leads to follow, Fitzgerald decided to check it out. Fitzgerald took three others with him and took no chances. When the room was pointed out to him, the men burst in with guns drawn on the Wilcoxes.

Mrs. Wilcox threw a small package into a cubby hole as Fitzgerald burst into the room. It turned out to be a small amount of diamond. Additionally, three revolvers, dynamite and bottle of chloroform were found during the search. The Wilcoxes were on the way to a police station.

Buoyed by the arrest and the items found, Fitzgerald and the other officers went around the corner to where the Wrights were known to stay. Fitzgerald have been given another tip, this one from a mailman that noted that the men often returned home in the early morning hours and always sober. The fact that they were not drunk was suspicious to him.

Fitzgerald posted a patrolman at the front of the boarding house to guard against escape from the windows. The remaining men pushed into the hallway where they encountered a surprised John Wright. Newspapers described him as tall and pretty. He was easily arrested.

As John Wright was being taken into custody, Fitzgerald noticed a woman running up the stairs. Following her, he burst in on Ed Wright. Wright, with gun in hand, was attempting to make an escape via the window but noticing the patrolman and a gun pointed at him, thought better of it.

Fitzgerald made to grab Ed Wright. Wright fired on him from point blank range. The bullets hit Fitzgerald in the heart. He is rumored to have said, "I'm finished", before falling to the floor dead. The trailing police officer wasted no time firing. Wright hit the floor, apparently subdued but still alive.

Ed Wright wasn't finished though. He had a gun stashed under the dresser. Reaching under it while the police were distracted, he came up firing wildly. The police were stunned, but unhurt by the volley, they recovered quickly. Ed Wright was struck by two bullets and this time stayed down.

A search of the room turned up more chloroform and dynamite as well as some cheap jewelry. The gang wouldn't be identified until a full three days later. The Wright brothers were Ed and Jack Biddle. Walter Dorman was Wilcox. The Chloroform gang was apprehended and in jail, except for Ed, who was recovering from his injuries in Mercy Hospital.

The women were also identified. They weren't wives after all, but women picked up during the gang's exploits. Mrs. Wright was Jessie Bodine and Mrs. Wilcox was Jennie Siefert, a burlesque chorus girl who had recently left her husband.

9

Ed Biddle recovered from his injuries quickly and joined his brother and Dorman in the Allegheny County jail. Dorman took no time in confessing and blamed Kahney's murder on the. Brothers.

The trial happened quickly. Dorman testified against the brothers in exchange for a life in prison sentence. Oddly, Ed and Jack were not tried for Paddy Fitzgerald's murder, only for Grocer Kahney's. The jury took no time in convicting the Biddle brothers and the judge sentenced them to execution by hanging.

In those days, hangings were conducted right in the jail yard. Ed was sentenced to hang on February 14, 1902, with his brother Jack following him to the noose two days later. However, the newspapers noted that neither seemed too worried about the sentence.

The warden of the prison was Peter Soffel. He was known to be lax. In fact, an escape had occurred ten years earlier by a murderer who was also awaiting execution. Mr. Soffel's wife, Katherine, lived with him in the warden's quarters on Ross Street.

Katherine is described as homely. A picture published of her shows sad, sunken eyes with thin lips. She is wearing tight collared dress with lace and her hair is pulled up and bushy. A newspaper reported that Mrs. Soffel would visit the Biddle brothers' cell, bringing them delicacies such as fruit and reading them bible passages.

Katherine Soffel

Warden Soffel responded by declaring that Katherine should not be impeded in any way. She should have full run of the prison as she was accustomed to and talk to whomever she wished and deliver anything she wished without question or interference.

Seduced by Ed Biddle's charm and taken by his handsomeness, Mrs. Soffel began a clandestine love affair with the doomed man. Some of the items she chose to deliver without interference were saws.

As she read aloud from the bible, the condemned men were sawing through the bars. They hid their handywork with shoe polish. Mrs. Soffel's bible came in handy in transmitting messages as well. Katherine would mark passages and leave it for Ed and Jack to read.

In the early morning hours of January 29, 1902, the Biddle brothers made their escape. Jack, feigning stomach cramps, lured one of the night guards to his cell. Jack snatched the unsuspecting guard up and pinned him against the bars. Ed, emerging from his cell, jammed a gun into his back.

Katherine had smuggled the guns to the brothers a night earlier. Jack nonchalantly kicked the bars loose from his cell and the two brothers tossed the guard over the rail to the floor, 16 feet below. A second guard was shot in the hip and a third complied with the brothers' orders and surrendered. Morning employees would arrive to find all three guards locked up.

Ed and Jack met Katherine in the warden's quarters. Mr. Soffel was sound asleep. He had spent the night drinking at an event. The Biddles dressed in the warden's clothes and the three conspirators emerged onto Ross Street into a driving snowstorm, free with just two weeks to the execution date.

Warden Soffel would awake confused, shocked, and embarrassed. He thought his wife was headed to visit relatives. He was informed that she never arrived nor was expected. He then suspected the killers had kidnapped her.

The guards then explained the facts of life to him and the worst kept secret of Katherine's infatuation with Ed Biddle. Soffel would next surmise that his wife must have chloroformed him and that is why he did not hear the escape. He would soon resign.

The Biddles case was assigned to Charley "Buck" McGovern. With Paddy Fitzgerald dead and buried, the young detective had taken over his case. Buck enlisted two other detectives, Al Swinehart and John Roach. The hunt for the fugitives was on and the legend would grow.

The Biddles admitted they did not want to take Katherine with them, but she was insistent that she would not leave Ed. For all the planning and excellent execution of the escape, there did not seem to be much forward thinking of what would come next.

What came next, is the three stepped out into a blinding snowstorm. The weather would slow their flight, giving time for the police to piece together what happened and begin the chase. The Biddles showed no urgency to put distance between them and the law either nor to avoid detection.

The Pittsburgh Courthouse no longer serves as a prison but is relatively unchanged from the time of the jailbreak.

The group was first seen in Allegheny City, present day northside of Pittsburgh. From there they made their way to Perrysville, a little community outside of Pittsburgh. In the village, they were spotted several times and the newspapers at this time were spreading their descriptions and the story. Ed stopped into the local hotel to buy sandwiches.

Making their way to the outskirts of town, they broke into the stables of a local farm and stole a black mare with a blaze of white, named Flora. They hitched it to a sleigh and set off through the thick snow covering at night.

Over an entire day after breaking out of prison, the fugitives were finally making an earnest escape. They pointed their sleigh north and travelled throughout the cold night. In these days, if you could make it to Canada, you were free. Everyone's best guess is that was where the trio was heading.

They made it to Butler, about 70 miles north of Pittsburgh by morning. They were half frozen and the horse dead tired after carrying them that distance in the cold. The Biddles and Mrs. Soffel stopped to warm up and rest the horse at a signal office for the local pipeline in Butler.

There were not many telephones yet in Pittsburgh, but two organizations did have them. One was the pipeline company, and the signal operator used his phone to call the other organization, the railroad office in Pittsburgh. He asked them to get the police, because the three fugitives that they were looking for were now sitting in his office.

The police were summoned but were not exactly quick to begin the pursuit. The case was Charlie "Buck" McCarthy's, and he was looking for revenge for the shooting of Patrick Fitzgerald during the original arrest. He grabbed two other officers and boarded a train from Pittsburgh to Butler.

By this point, the horse was rested, and the fugitives set off down New Castle Pike, which is now State Route 422. The signal operator decided to put a tail on the horse and sleigh. A tail in those days, was a guy on a horse. He rode in wide circles around the Biddles to try and not raise suspicion. He had no means of communicating his position but hoped to ascertain the direction that the trio was heading.

The signal operator picked up Buck in the other officers at the train station in a horse and wagon. Buck climbed up front, while the other two were left to stuff themselves uncomfortably in the wagon. The posse set out in the last known direction, hoping for a little luck.

Luck was on the officers' side. They nearly ran straight into the Biddles in their pursuit. Spotting them off in the distance, Buck relayed his instructions to the signal operator. He was to get as close as possible without slowing down. When Buck gave him the signal, he was to pull the horses to an abrupt stop to the side, allowing Buck and the officers to gain cover.

The signal operator had no military or police training. Buck gave him the signal and the operator pulled the horses to a stop perfectly next to some cover. Buck hopped out with the officers scrambling out of the wagon as fast as possible. Grabbing cover, Buck steadied and aimed his rifle at the oncoming sleigh.

Buck shouted to the Biddles to surrender! They, of course, refused his offer. Instead, the Biddle jumped up and began firing wildly in the still moving sleigh. Their aim, hindered by the motion, missed badly. Buck on the other hand had cover and was a good shot with his rifle.

He fired, striking both brothers and knocking them from the moving sleigh. They landed in the snow, turning it red with mortal wounds they had been delivered. Mrs. Soffel distraught from the realization that she would lose the love of her life, Ed Biddle, decided to shoot herself. Perhaps, in the stress of the situation, she did not consider options very well as she managed to only shoot her in the shoulder – not a mortal wound.

With Flora still running and Mrs. Soffel still positioned in the sleigh, Buck shouted to his officers to, "Shoot the horse!" The officers looked at him as if he were mad. They did manage to get the horse to stop, and Flora was eventually returned to her stable, relatively unscathed.

Mrs. Soffel was taken to the hospital in Butler. The Biddles, still alive, were taken to the Butler prison and doctors were summoned. Upon quick examination, both were predicted to die within hours.

Butler County Courthouse

As the Biddles lay in the cell dying, they began to relate the details of their escape to anyone that would listen, which is why the story still exists to this day. Meanwhile, news had spread quickly of the Biddles' capture and impending deaths. Nearly a thousand people, most of them women, descended on the prison to get a last look at the handsome brothers who had made a daring escape.

The next morning, the Biddles' coffins were loaded onto a railroad car bound for the city morgue in Pittsburgh. 21 officers were posted to guard the morgue, having heard of the previous night's mob. It was not enough. Thousands again poured into the morgue hoping for one last glance at the handsome brothers who had made a daring escape.

The Biddles were laid out at a local funeral home. Pittsburgh police were on hand to hopelessly control the throngs. People came from far and wide to stream past the caskets, holding the handsome brothers who had made a daring escape.

A few onlookers became confused and invaded the next-door neighbor's house by accident. He was not amused when they demanded to see the Biddles. A distraught young woman, that had never met Jack Biddle, penned a heart-breaking letter to him and then committed suicide.

Mrs. Soffel recovered from her shoulder wound and was brought back to the Allegheny County Prison, this time as an inmate. She was given a sentence of two years as it was uncommon to hold female prisoners at that time.

Upon her release, she attempted to sell her story. After two years though, the hubbub had died off and no one was buying. She worked as a seamstress to support herself and died a few years after.

A new, hard-nosed warden replaced Soffel. After all, this was the second prison escape that happened on his watch.

Mrs. Soffel may still roam the old prison today. Local tour company, Haunted Pittsburgh, claims you may catch a glimpse of her ghostly form in the windows along Ross Street, still pining for her true love.

3 Pittsburgh's Chinatown – Battles Won and Lost

Children scampered and played on the tree lined streets. Adults sat around drinking tea and playing mahjong, swapping stories in the dialect of Southern China. Shops were lined with exotic silks and satins as well as savory and sweet delights. This was Pittsburgh's Chinatown at the turn of the 20th century.

Pittsburgh's Chinatown was not as large as those in New York City, San Francisco or Washington, DC. The heart of Chinatown was on Second and Third Avenues between Ross and Grant streets, stretching to the river before the construction of the Boulevard of the Allies.

Still, it was a dynamic hub of tradition, culture, and commerce. Pittsburgh's Chinatown began forming in the 1870's and 1880's. Pittsburgh was a stop or gateway to the west, where jobs awaited building the railroad or mining for gold. Arriving from New York City, many found the growing industrial center of Pittsburgh held as much promise as there was further west.

The Beaver Falls Cutlery Company was one of the first large-scale employers. The company reported hiring 70 Chinese laborers. As more people arrived, they built businesses to create a self-sufficient community, including grocers, restaurants, and other retail businesses.

Shopkeepers lived above their businesses and children grew up working in the stores. As the community grew, new arrivals, Chinese fraternal organizations, or tongs, soon followed. And they didn't always get along.

Tong translates to hall. They were like chambers of commerce and social organization wrapped into one. They provided support to businesses and individuals like, helping to resolve disputes or those that needed a helping hand.

Pittsburgh's tongs were set up by the larger organizations in New York City. Two tongs set up shop in Pittsburgh, the On Leong Labor Organization and the Hip Sing Tong. They competed for members in Pittsburgh and other cities, and the rivalry grew as each tried to gain an upper hand in the burgeoning community.

On Leong was more successful, growing to 800 members as compared to 600 for Hip Sing. However, Hip Sing had powerful allies in New York City that they could call on for support. Both protected Chinese immigrants and labor force from discrimination which was rampant by the American workforce.

As the Tong's power grew, there were also allegations of extortion, drugs and even assassins for hire. All businesses in the Pittsburgh community, big or small, were "required" to join a tong and competition was fierce.

Tongs made loans to businesses, posted bail for members that were arrested, and would even pay for a burial. There are 300 graves in a section of Homewood Cemetery that were paid for by the Chinese Cemetery Company.

They also were guardians of culture, producing parades, festivals and other celebrations that kept many traditions of the Chinese people. In 1921, the neighborhood was recognized as one of the busiest places in Pittsburgh.

That year also marked the beginning of the destruction of the community. In 1921, the city began construction of the Boulevard of the Allies, which cut off nearly a third of the original area. When the ramp was complete it cast a shadow over Second Avenue and the vibrancy of the neighborhood.

Still Chinatown grew, reaching 700 people and more than 25 businesses in 1925, its apex. It was so crowded and prosperous that a local cab company stationed a dispatcher at the corner of Second Avenue and Grant Street. The community was isolated from the rest of the city. Most residents did not mix with other Pittsburghers as only a few were able to speak English.

A delicate peace between the tongs reigned until 1927. George Lee, a rising leader in the On Leong organization would help set things off in Pittsburgh's Chinatown. The George Lee name seems to be infamous in Pittsburgh, as a different person with that name will rise to be the Vice King of Pittsburgh later in this book.

This particular George Lee decided to switch allegiances, forming a rival Hip Sing faction. While Lee was stirring things up here, the Tong Wars erupted nationwide in 1928 between the On Leong and Hip Sing, bringing violence.

After shootings killed 4 people in New York and Washington, Willie Yat, the unofficial mayor of Chinatown, appealed to city officials to step up police protection in the neighborhood. Yat spoke English where most of the neighborhood did not.

Two detectives were sent to assess the situation. The report stated that everything was "serene" between Ross and Grant Streets and Second and Third Avenue. Not soon after, a young On Leong worker was shot on Ross Street on the way to his job at the laundromat. He survived his injuries and police did catch the shooter. Not surprisingly, the assailant was affiliated with the Hip Sing organization, but not from Pittsburgh. He was hired gun from New York City.

Pittsburgh avoided the worst of the bloodshed. One Hundred people were killed during the Tong Wars nationwide. George Lee would not survive to see the end. Most predicted he would die with his boots on in a hail of gunfire. Instead, he succumbed in bed to a brain illness in 1927 at the age of 43. There was no word if his boots were on in bed.

The Tong Wars brought increased scrutiny from the city. Planning projects for the growth of the city brought large scale development to the edges of Chinatown further constricting it. Children brought up in the neighborhood began going to city schools, learning English, becoming "*Americanized*", and ultimately going on to college.

The Great Depression accelerated the decline. It seems that the city did not care that a once prosperous community was facing a desperate fight for survival. Many families fled to the suburbs, starting cultural enclaves in other areas that still exist today.

Even families that left for other opportunity returned throughout the years to visit the remaining businesses. The assimilation into the city continued as well. In 1940, to "teach the children of Chinatown American ways and Christianity", Santa Claus visited the neighborhood for the first time. Fred Young, a volunteer at the Mt. Washington Mission, played Santa, riding in an open car through the streets.

By 1959 only three families were left. Yet to this day, there are two buildings remaining in the neighborhood that date back to the glory days of Chinatown. The most recognizable is the Chinatown Inn Restaurant on Third Avenue. Before it was transformed into a restaurant, it was a grocery store. Before that, it was the social hall for the On Leong Fraternal Organization. When you enjoy a meal, be sure to enjoy sitting in the history of the founding of this community.

The second is a building on Court Place which used to be 517 Second Avenue. It currently houses a Chinese takeout restaurant. The Hip Sing headquarters were once in this building, and they are still listed as the owners of the building today.

Next time you are in this area envision it as a vibrant, prosperous, and energetic community full of culture, heritage, and dreams. Look past the imposing government buildings and the roadway, and see storefronts erupting in sights, sounds, smells, and most of all people.

That was Pittsburgh's Chinatown.

4 **Grant's Hill**

Pittsburgh is in Allegheny County and the Allegheny River flows from the North to meet up with the Monongahela River and form the Ohio River at the "forks of the Ohio", now Point State Park.

The name Allegheny is attributed to the Lenape word oolikhanna, which translates to beautiful stream. The river was named first and was originally spelled Allghene. The county came much later and was named for the river.

Before colonial settlement this area was settled by several Native American tribes, including the Iroquois, Shawnee, Mingo, and the Lenape that were also known as the Delaware People. The tribes considered the Allegheny River to be all one river that being the Ohio.

The surrounding areas of Pittsburgh were fertile hunting grounds and there were agreements amongst the tribes for this territory. Pittsburgh was a spiritual center with meetings and ceremonies taking place at the Point.

Pittsburgh was also a burial ground, and an ancient one. Before the Lenape came to the area, the natural topography of Pittsburgh lent itself to the mound builders of Pre-Columbian cultures.

If you stand on Grant Street today, the main government and business corridor in Pittsburgh, you are actually standing on an ancient burial ground. As you look toward the fountain in Point State Park you can see the incline that Pittsburgh's downtown was built upon.

Grant Street is named for British Major General James Grant. Grant led colonial troops against the French Garrison at Ft. Duquesne in present day Point State Park during the French and Indian War. He failed miserably, losing a good deal of his men. He was captured during the fight.

Now, picture yourself 30 feet higher. Before this was Grant Street, it was called Grant's Hill and it jeopardized the future development of the city. It was difficult to traverse, and the planners of the city wanted flatter ground to build out the sprawling metropolis.

After several aborted attempts, excavation was finally completed in 1912 at a cost of $800,000. During excavation, however, workers found that this was no ordinary hill. As they dug it out, they found several Native Americans burials.

Several were reburied at the shared cemetery of Trinity Episcopal Cathedral and First Presbyterian Church on Sixth Avenue. Trinity was built on an old hilltop cemetery and its churchyard contains some of the oldest graves of French, British, Colonial and Native American leaders.

The excavation is rumored to have discovered something strange as well. Amongst the burials, several remains of nine-foot and more in size were also discovered. These ancient giants were not reburied in Pittsburgh. Rather, legend has it that they were spirited away to the Smithsonian Museum to be studied under great security.

Who were these super tall pre-historic humans? Lenape legend tells of a great warrior tribe that inhabited the area along the river called the Allegewi. This may have been translated from the Lanape word Talligewi, meaning "ancient ones".

The Allegewi were skilled fighters, but also were of high skill and intelligence. They had great fortifications with high walls and lived in organized villages. They were mound builders and were spread from the banks of the Mississippi through the Ohio river valley.

The Lenape migration myth tells of the tribe originating in the western part of North America and travelling east in search of new land. When they encountered the Allegewi, the Lenape asked for permission to settle in the area. The Lenape were amazed by the size of the Allegewi people, remarking that even the women outmatched the Lenape men in height and girth.

The Allegewi denied the Lenape permission to settle in its lands but did grant them safe passage through their territory on the way to other lands. At the same time, the Iroquois were pushing south into the Allegewi's lands by force.

As the Lenape were making their way through the territory, the Allegewi supposedly reneged on their promise of safety and began to sporadically hassle the Lenape. The Allegewi's fighting prowess preceded them.

The Lenape were aware of the stories. The Mohawks had come upon the Allegewi in their mountain fortresses and were nearly beaten to extinction. A group of 100 Allegewi held off a much larger Seneca force, defending their borders and then chasing the routed Senecas back to New York.

The Lenape had taken a purposeful southern route to avoid the Iroquois, but now had to make a decision. To counter the strength of the Allegewi, the Lenape joined forces with the Iroquois and a great battle was begun.

The combined forces were up to what was before an insurmountable challenge. They were able to broach the walls of the Allegewi settlements and drive the people from the territory. The surviving Allegewi migrated south and were absorbed by southern tribes. In particular, the Cherokee tribe, known for its strength as well, believe they were descended from the Allegewi.

It is not just in Native American lore that a tribe of giants appear. Captain John Smith, he of Pocahontas fame, recounts a journey to the Susquehanna River in central Pennsylvania where he met a tribe, likely the Allegewi, of men and women of large stature and superior fighting and building skills.

The Smithsonian never published any findings of the skeletons that were supposedly transferred to them. It may just be legend, or the exhumed skeletons may be locked up in the underground vaults below the museum.

In Pittsburgh, I have met with a person who believes he was descended from the ancient mound builders. He was tall in stature though not reaching nine feet. The Allegewi stories may be hard to believe today, however, it is plausible that giants once ruled this area.

If they moved south into the protection of the mountains and forests, they may have given rise to another legend, that of Bigfoot. A small coal patch town southeast of Pittsburgh has reported several sightings and there are many reports from the wilds of West Virginia. The Lenape believe the Allegewi moved to their favorite land just south of the area in present day Kentucky.

Stories of the Allegewi continue to disappear with time and their existence may continue to move into myth in the future if further evidence does not surface. However, the river, county and certainly the Allegheny Mountains seem to have taken their name from this legendary people.

As for the Lenape, their alliance with the Iroquois proved fruitful. They settled across Pennsylvania and Delaware. The lands around Pittsburgh were shared hunting grounds between multiple tribes and the banks of the three rivers were a place of fellowship until settlers pushed the Native Americans out of the area.

In 2018, members of the Lenape and other tribes returned to what is now Point State Park as part of a historical celebration by the Fort Pitt Blockhouse and Museum. A fire was lit, and dancing and fellowship once again brought the ground to life and filled the air with electricity of another time.

Gone, But Let's Not Forget

These next three stories are labeled as infamous. The locations are not there anymore. They were older buildings and were removed to make room for new development or in the case of the Court Bar – a parking lot.

Though the places are gone – the stories are not. In the case of these three stories, Pittsburgh might like to forget. However, good, or bad, these stories represent a time, a place and even a lesson for the future.

5 Pittsburgh's Longest Serving Brothel

At the time of this writing, the building at 212-214 Blvd. of the Allies was in the process of being demolished along with three others to make room for a new development.

It is difficult to see a building with so much history and character cease to exist. In economic development, you weigh the chance to save what is important piece of history against what could be a future historical structure and new economic driver of a community.

The red brick building at 214 Blvd. of the Allies has been empty for several years. It is not easy to adapt to other uses, and the time empty has left it in severe disrepair. The roof is leaking, and environmental damage has added to the issues the building already was experiencing.

The building was constructed in 1860 and both truth and legend have manufactured an incredible history – one that will live on even though the building is no more. Before demolition, it still featured black railing, lanterns, and corks in the window.

The last tenant was Papa J's Downtown Restaurant. It served up Italian until it closed in 2013 after problems with a gas line in the building. The menu was still there as if it was going to open at any minute. However, if you peered in the windows, you would have seen that the famous bar had been dismantled and there wasn't anything but debris remaining in the front room.

Pittsburgh's Young Preservationists noted that the buildings were of the few remaining civil war era structures in downtown Pittsburgh and offer a "valuable glimpse into pre-industrialized Pittsburgh. It is remarkable that they survived major developments, particularly the construction of the PPG complex, which is across the street.

The building has held many previous roles. It was purported to be a stop on the Underground Railroad, a safe haven for former slaves as they travelled north. However, most people know it as one of Pittsburgh's longest running brothels, serving clients until 1937.

Dolly Cavanaugh bought the building in the early 1900's with a simple purpose in mind. She transformed the 10 bedrooms into a thriving business serving Pittsburgh's elite. She was given the title of Madam Dolly and managed to operate the bordello for more than thirty years in the prime spot.

How did such a business survive right out in the open? Dolly checked in her clientele in a record, an early black book. Each visitor was checked against a signature and if you were not of means, you were bounced out the door.

The brothel was not for the working class. Madam Dolly charged double the going rate for her girls. One dollar at the time when the standard was fifty cents. And if you are catering to the elite clientele, you have the protection to skirt the law, especially if you have documentation that would expose or embarrass said power brokers.

It is obvious that Dolly had a good business that generated money. However, it wasn't without hassles. Dolly may have been protected from the law, but a jealous husband is another story. One evening, one of Dolly's girls was in an upstairs bedroom. Her husband burst into the brothel and up the stairs to the room. He stabbed his wife several times, killing her on the spot.

This incident would later lead to paranormal sightings in the ladies' room and other areas by patrons of the restaurant. In fact, the bar was listed as haunted and recommended as a place where an individual might have a sighting. A partial apparition of a woman was often seen by guests, most often by women.

Dolly ran the brothel until 1934. In that year, she sold the building, and it went legit as a boarding house, albeit a seedy one. The boarding house operated until 1979, when the Zeliesko brothers bought the building.

The brothers restored the rooms back to Dolly's time with woodwork and mirrors dating to the period. They opened Tramp's, the Grande Olde Saloon. It was heralded as 'friendly, classy Downtown bar and four-star restaurant, with a naughty past.

Lore and facts get mixed when it comes to the bar area. Tramp's installed a magnificent bar back that was once the headboard to Mary Frick's bed. Ms. Frick was a notable socialite and member of a powerful Pittsburgh family. However, by the time Papa J's opened, the story had changed to be the headboard of Madame Dolly.

The black book is legend as well. The book was supposedly found in a false ceiling in her bed chamber. However, patrons of Tramps could peruse a mahogany box that contained 1,000 numbered cards containing the signatures of Dolly's clientele.

One thing is for certain, the book or the box of cards disappeared when Tramp's moved out. They have never been released publicly, creating speculation that they would incriminate prominent families to this day.

Papa J's Centro was opened by the Troiani family in 1994. The headboard bar back would remain, and they continued to pay homage to Madame Dolly, serving the Madame's Blood E. Mary cocktail.

Red lanterns hung from the top of the building – an homage to its former use?

Papa J's Centro did a thriving downtown business with the business lunch crowd and the curious evening crowd sampling some of the best food and drink in the city. Sure, the building was never optimal as a restaurant, but the owners and staff made it work until Veteran's Day of 2013.

As the annual Veteran's Day parade was marching down the Blvd. of the Allies, a gas leak would bring down the building for good. Michael Troiani hoped to reopen the restaurant after the leak was fixed, but on December 5th, he announced it the Papa J's Centro would be closed for good.

In May of 2014, Fred Peters Auctioneers listed for sale fixtures and contents of the former Papa J's. The ornate woodwork, stained glass windows, an oak claw-foot sideboard, cast-iron claw-foot bathtub as well as restaurant-ready appliance, utensils and furnishings were offered for sale.

The highlight of the auction though was the headboard. The auctioneers promoted it as a notorious piece of Pittsburgh history, once belonging to Madame Dolly Cavanaugh. There is no indication as to where the headboard ended up after the auction. However, the legend lives on, and the question remains if Dolly's clientele will ever be publicly revealed.

6 Pittsburgh's First Bank Robbery

No one is quite sure of when Joseph Pluymart and Herman Emmons arrived in Pittsburgh, but they would set off a series of events that would drive change in the fledgling community and leave their mark in its history.

On the night of April 6, 1818, Pluymart and Emmons would let themselves into the Farmers and Mechanics Bank at 226 Fourth Avenue and make off with $100,000 in bank notes and an additional $3,000 in gold and silver. The bank robbery will forever be remembered as the first in Pittsburgh.

Pluymart and Emmons are said to have come to Pittsburgh from New York. The papers called them Yankees. Emmons may have operated a store there. Pluymart was likely a gambler and con-artist and was called "Doc". He may have passed himself off as a doctor when he first arrived.

Not much is known of their time in the city before the robbery. The pair were in residence for several months prior to the caper, as was confessed by Emmons after he was caught. Both men were described as of slight build and well-dressed.

There was no police force in Pittsburgh at this time. The city employed watchmen. In the classic sense, these men were stationed throughout the city and would announce the time and weather as well as declare, "all is well", on the hour throughout the night. They would pass the intervals in lounging in their watch boxes.

Pluymart and Emmons had noticed that the key to the back door of the Farmer's and Mechanics Bank was hung carelessly on the watch box and that the watchmen was more concerned with warming himself at the stove than watching for potential wrongdoing.

The pair snatched the key and let themselves into the bank. They surveyed the inside and found that the vault doors were locked. Taking measurements of the keyholes, Pluymart decided to make keys that could open the locks.

They replaced the key to the watch box so as not to arouse suspicions and went about the task of fashioning the keys. Over the period of a few months, the pair would visit the bank five additional times, refining the measurements and perfecting the keys.

On each occasion, they would slip the key off the watch box without the watchman's notice and let themselves into the bank. Emmons found a $50 note carelessly left in a cash drawer rather than the vault on one visit. He snatched it and showed it to Pluymart. Pluymart chastised his partner to put it back or the whole plot would be foiled.

On the evening of April 6, the men slipped in and opened the outer and inner vault doors. They cleaned it out of everything. The bank had $100,000 in bank notes, approximately $3,000 in gold and silver as well as some personal property. They replaced the key to the watch box and headed to the river to make an escape.

On the morning of April 7, Morgan Neville, the bank's cashier, unlocked the bank as usual. He went to the vault and found the outer door closed but unlocked. This was odd. He threw open the doors and found the inner doors wide open and the vault empty.

Neville immediately summoned the directors to report the crime. A report reached them that two men had been seen boarding a skiff on the Monongahela River headed towards the Ohio River. One of the bank's directors, William Lecky, wasted no time. He boarded his own boat with two other men and rowed furiously after them.

Lecky caught up to the two men on the Ohio River in Wheeling, West Virginia. He performed a search of the persons and the boat but found no evidence of the robbery. He remained suspicious and set off down river ahead of Pluymart and Emmons.

Arriving in Cincinnati, Ohio, he dispatched one of his men to wait for Pluymart and Emmons and search the pair again when they arrived. He never got a chance as the two were captured by Ohio authorities in Neville about 30 miles north of Cincinnati.

During the capture, Emmons arm was broken. Pluymart and Emmons were taken to jail in Cincinnati and the extradition wrangling started. The governor of Ohio signed the order, but the people of Cincinnati did not want the men returned to Pittsburgh and refused to honor it. Lecky would argue before the local authorities for the return, and the proceedings would drag on for two months.

That was plenty of time for Pluymart. He engineered an escape for Emmons and himself. Emmons, with a broken arm, slowed down Pluymart on the run. They would split up with Pluymart heading north towards Canada.

Emmons was caught not soon after this. Injured and tired, he gave himself up and was returned to Pittsburgh. Once there, he struck a deal with Pittsburgh authorities. If he could avoid a jail term, he would take them to where the money was hidden.

Potential stash location on the river outside of Beaver, PA

Under cover of night, to not arouse the suspicions of would-be bandits, Emmons brought a group of Pittsburgh citizens 'of the highest reproach' to a rock formation on the shore of the Ohio, just below Beaver, Pennsylvania.

There nearly all of the $100,000 in bank notes were said to have been recovered though damaged by the wetness. Some of the silver was also recovered still in the original bank boxes. Evidently, the men had hidden their booty, taking just enough for their immediate needs. The area became known to river pilots as Pluymart's rock.

Emmons' testimony also cleared a third person that was being held under suspicion of the robbery. His name was never mentioned in the papers. A massive manhunt was organized for Pluymart and papers in New York City ran articles on the robbery, the daring escape and the dogged pursuit of Lecky.

Puymart would turn up in Ogdenburg, New York which sits on the border with Ontario, Canada. There was no formal extradition between the United States and Canada. IF you crossed the border, you were free.

The authorities in Ogdenburgh were elated to catch such a high-profile criminal. They dashed off a letter to Pittsburgh informing them of the arrest. A second letter was dispatched a few days later saying that Pluymart had escaped but was retaken fifteen miles away and was back in jail.

Pluymart had $5,000 in banks notes on him as well as gold. When this news reached Emmons, it caught him by surprise. They took no gold with them and Pluymart had more bank notes on him than they left with. It seems Pluymart had made a stop at the secret cache before it was recovered.

Of great concern to the bank and in particularly Neville, the cashier, was a gold medal that was still missing. The medal had been awarded to General Daniel Morgan for his bravery at the Battle of Cowpens during the American Revolution. Neville was the General's grandson and came into ownership of the medal which he stored in the bank's vault.

Emmons believed the medal to be lost to the river. He said that during the pursuit they had dumped a bag containing some of the loot as well as the medal over the side of the boat. It was now beyond recovery at the bottom of the Ohio. However, Pluymart may have made an unknowing switch at the hideaway, later recovering the medal and melting it down. It was worth a significant 29 guineas at the time, approximately half a pound in gold.

Pluymart was returned to Pittsburgh and stood trial. He was sentenced to three years in the newly constructed Western Penitentiary. It would not hold him long.

An expert in key making, I'm not sure any jail could have held Pluymart. He escaped by fashioning a copper key from copper spouts in the prison yard. He and another prisoner of 'extraordinary size and strength' were allowed walks in the yard each day for their health.

Once the key was made, they tied it to a stick and extended it to the open keyhole, unlocking it. The accomplice then ripped it from its hinges. There was no night watch at the time and the prisoners easily made their way through the yard. To scale the outer wall, the pair built an impromptu ladder from some boxes, stacking them in a spiral fashion.

They lowered themselves down by a rope fashioned from their sheets. The escape again put Pluymart in the nation's papers. This time he would disappear for ten years.

The following year in 1819, Farmers and Mechanics Banks was no more. They summoned an emergency and mandatory meeting for all directors at the courthouse. The papers then published a resolution from the meeting announcing the dissolvement and disbursement of the remaining assets. The resolution cited the previous year's robbery and loss as the reason behind the closing.

It is important to note that the exact sums lost to the robbery or recovered from Emmons confession were never officially accounted and reported. Sums varied widely. The bank notes listed as $100,000 seems to be accurate. The bank may not have recovered as much as reported, however.

The real discrepancies seem to be with the silver and gold held. In the resolution it was alluded that a significant portion may not have been recovered. This loss of funds as well as the general loss in business from the heavily reported robbery doomed the bank to just five years of service.

The location remained a bank. The Bank of Pittsburgh, formed a few years before Farmers and Mechanic, built a new banking house on the lot, which is one of the oldest lots in Pittsburgh. The new building would be a shining example of Greek Revival architecture with 30-foot-tall Corinthian columns. Despite its historic status as the oldest bank west of the Allegheny Mountains, the building would be torn down in 1944. It is now a parking garage.

The watch was ended as well because of the robbery. The city hired its first paid city policeman and gradually added to the force. The old watch boxes were turned into light posts. The force would continue the practice of announcing the time, weather and if all is well. They were also responsible for lighting the lamps.

The early force was only slightly more effective than the watch that replaced. An editorial remarked that they spend more time drilling on the bluff where Duquesne University now sits rather than catching crooks.

After a review by the prison board, they noted defects in the construction of Western Penitentiary that contributed to the escape. Several changes were made to the cell doors to restrict access and a night watch was installed.

Both Lacky and Neville were elected in later years to the position of Sheriff of Allegheny County. Lacky certainly proved himself adept at pursuing criminals as well as arguing law because of the robbery.

As for Pluymart, his time on the run was fruitful. He got in with a gang that was more adept at crime than his previous accomplice. During a two-year period, before he resurfaces in 1828, the gang stole and conned $80,000. As they were rounded up, Pluymart is again put on a trial.

He uses the defense of mental and physical anguish that was the result of being arrested four times, standing trial, and running from the law. The journalists covering the trial remarked that this is the first time that mental anguish caused by committing crime was used as a defense. If he would have just served his prison term, there would be no anguish.

Turns out Pluymart needn't worry. While he was on the run, he had managed to secure admittance to the Masons in Philadelphia. On his behalf, Masonic leadership appealed to the outgoing Governor John Andrew Shulze. The sixth governor of Pennsylvania delivered a clemency order on his last day granting Pluymart a pardon for the robbery and his subsequent escapes.

Citing his most commendable service to the community and with letters of endorsement from citizens in Philadelphia, Cleveland, and New York, Pluymart was a free man. The people of Pittsburgh were by no surprise outraged by the announcement. "A man's skills in the art of villainy have been used as a means of exciting sympathy."

Pluymart marries and settles down in Connecticut, raising a family. His escapades on April 6, 1818, led to the establishment of Pittsburgh's police force, improvements in incarceration, the ruin of an early banking institution and a story that is still celebrated more than 200 years later.

Altogether, Joseph Pluymart appears to have been as accomplished a scoundrel as ever graced the annals of American crime.

7 Pittsburgh's Most Infamous Bar and One of Its Most Creative Criminals

In Pittsburgh's history, there have been many infamous nightlife spots, but the Showboat Club which once stood at 125 Fourth Avenue had a legendary ten-year run that ended with its manager thrown in jail and its contents auctioned.

Before the Showboat, the space housed a non-descript confectionary store. It would be transformed into a members-only plush night spot with oak beams, a walnut bar, paneled walls and thick red carpeting.

The Showboat Club was founded in 1963 by two state legislators, several people on the city government payroll and Antonio Ripepi, an alleged underworld figure. The liquor license was awarded to a nonprofit, the Italian American Professional and Businessmen's Association. As such, it was considered a fraternal club not a bar which meant you had to be a member to have a drink.

This did not dissuade non-members from enjoying themselves. The club was raided on three separate occasions and fined for serving alcohol to non-members. On one such occasion, an undercover officer was admitted by the bouncer, and sat at the bar sipping cocktails until the rest of the officers arrived. All this when membership was only $25.00.

The club signed a ten-year lease at the location and by all accounts was doing well. That is, until about 90 days before the lease was about to expire, when the club stopped paying its $1,200 per month rent.

At the same time, a struggle within the Association emerged. Geno Chiarelli made the claim that he was elected President of the organization but was not recognized by the rival faction led by the club's manager, Sonny Peters.

Advertisement for the Showboat Club

Chiarelli was not a person to be trifled with, and Peters took the step of locking him out of the club. A former Marine and general contractor, Chiarelli was tough. He was also a member of the Pittsburgh Family that would pull off two of the most creative heists in Pittsburgh history.

The disagreement would land in court and additional creditors would emerge, everything from meat purveyors to the electric company. Eight lawyers representing various parties battled in front of Common Pleas Judge Robert A. Doyle.

In May of 1972, the Showboat was put into receivership and a sheriff sale was planned. It would be delayed until November by various motions in judgements. The message did not reach the public however, people were still seen coming and going from the club with a few drinks in between.

The city raided the establishment again at the end of the month and found non-members imbibing as per usual. The city had seen enough. They arrested six Showboat employees, including Peters.

Peters failed to appear for court and when he did finally show, he used the defense that he was not on-duty during the night of the raid. A very unhappy Criminal Court Judge Robert Van der Voort didn't accept Peters excuses and set his bond at an exorbitant amount of $30,000. Peters, a father of six, could not make the bond and was sent to jail.

The Showboat's court proceedings dragged into the fall. Neither Chiarelli nor Peters could produce Association records declaring an election of officers. Peters could not even produce an accurate set of books. The Liquor Control Board revoked the Showboat's license, and the ornate furnishings were sold via auction to satisfy creditors.

The Showboat was sunk. The building would be demolished to make way for the PPG Place development which broke ground in 1981. The 'glass castle" as it is known in Pittsburgh was designed by Philip Johnson and opened for business in 1983 and 1984.

Chiarelli would emerge from the wreckage of the Showboat Club as a creative planner of million-dollar heists. The first took place on March 17, 1982, St. Patrick's Day and to this day was never solved.

At 11:30 p.m. on that day, two men ducked under an automatic gate as a Purolator armored truck was leaving to make a delivery to the airport. The men approached the night security guard, James Powers. They were wearing trench coats and dark glasses. They carried walkie talkies, flashlights, and FBI badges that they flashed.

They told Powers that they were from the FBI and that they had a good tip that Purolator was going to be robbed. Powers was carrying a shotgun and had a pistol in a holster. Before he knew what was happening, the two men had yanked the shotgun from his hand, spun him around and disarmed him of the pistol as well.

Powers was handcuffed, his feet were trussed and tape place over his eyes. The two men then opened the gate and radioed to their getaway car. As it pulled up, the men entered the vault area of the terminal and loaded thirty bags with bills ranging from $5 to $100. Loading them onto steel carts they packed them into the car. They sped away with $2.5 million without firing a shot.

It took 90 minutes for Powers to crawl to a phone. He randomly dialed a number and convinced the woman on the other end to call the police. When the real FBI arrived, they suspected that there had to be inside help.

The vault door was open for the thieves and the job was so smooth that they must have had insider information on schedules and what to take. $2.5 million was a princely sum, but the vault held $55 million at the time of the robbery.

Powers would be questioned extensively. He exclaimed that the vault was open as a truck was expected for a pickup. The money stolen was prepared for the next delivery. Powers would be cleared but was fired by Purolator. He would sue the company for wrongful termination and settled out of court.

The former Chief of Brentwood's Police, Robert Hartshorn, remarked, "a real wizard planned this one, that's for sure."

The case remains unsolved but resurfaced in 1990 during the huge racketeering trial in Pittsburgh. Chiarelli was on the stand for other crimes and informant testimony from the FBI linked Chiarelli to the 1982 heist.

Four years later in March of 1986, Chiarelli would pull off a second million-dollar heist. He and two others drilled into the concrete supported roof of a vault in the First Seneca Bank in Greensburg. They disconnected the alarms and made off with $2 million in antique weapons that a private collector stored at the bank.

Everything was going well, until they tried to sell the stolen goods. Transporting them to Tampa, they were arrested during an attempted sale to an insurance agent. The led police on a high-speed chase in their van, nearly striking a school bus, before they were caught.

Former First Seneca Bank

In court, the prosecution could not prove that Chiarelli was responsible for the theft, and he was charge for possession and transportation of stolen goods. The judge, citing the high-speed chase where Chiarelli was a passenger, sentenced him to a strict five years.

Chiarelli would appeal the sentence and won a reversal. He was resentenced to two years for the crime. This would be the beginning of far greater legal troubles for him.

In 1990, a grand jury brought charges under the Racketeer Influenced and Corrupt Organizations Act, commonly known as RICO. This would be the first RICO trial in Pittsburgh, and it ensnared nine men charged with operating a massive cocaine trafficking ring as well as the murder of Joseph Bertone in 1985.

The government's star witness was Joseph Rosa. Rosa was arrested on drug charges and turned informant to reduce his sentence. Rosa testified that he ran the Pittsburgh Family's drug business under the direction of Charles Porter.

Chiarelli was implicated as an enforcer under Porter, shaking down drug dealers for a percentage of their sales. Rosa also testified that he had told him that he supplied the weapon to kill Bertone. Bertone disappeared from a trucking company's lot and his body was never found.

Chiarelli was cleared of the Bertone murder but was found guilty on the drug charges. He was sentenced in January of 1991 to 22 years. He would serve nearly twenty years, gaining early release for good behavior. Ironically, he would end up serving double the years of his alleged boss, Porter.

Porter turned informant and reduced his sentence with information that brought down organized crime and drug traffickers across the country. He even notified the FBI about a planned hit on Rosa, who was now in the Witness Protection Program.

After Chiarelli's release, he lived with his son. He passed away in 2012. From the Showboat to two of the most daring million-dollar heists, he was one of the last wise guys of Pittsburgh.

The Rise of the Rackets and Prohibition

Pittsburgh had long been a corrupt town with the line between civic leader and criminal a blurry microcosm of characters mixing legitimate and illegitimate business practices, deliberate ignorance, or just plain incompetence.

Like many cities, the rackets started as loosely organized gangs. However, there were illegal speakeasies long before Prohibition was ratified by Pennsylvania. The state has always had a hand in controlling booze and profiting from it. This still exists today with the state-controlled liquor stores maintaining a monopoly hold on most alcohol.

In the late 1800s, the state instituted a prohibitively expensive license to open a tavern. The licenses essentially locked out many tavern owners and consolidated properties into the hands of the wealthy.

This practice continues to this day. Pennsylvania limits the number of liquor licenses available per county. This practice has created a lucrative third-party market for licenses, valuing them far greater than often the property itself in transactions between to two parties.

One would think that the state would have learned from the federal government. Not more than one hundred years earlier, small producers of whiskey started a rebellion over taxation policies from the fledgling nation.

Instead of outright rebellion, tavern keepers simply moved underground. As legend has it, the term "speakeasy" was coined by one such Pittsburgh entrepreneur, when she urged her loud patrons to "Speak easy boys", so as not to arouse the interests of the roving patrols.

The movement underground, meant the need to stay under the radar. These included supply of booze and protection from the authorities and other unscrupulous people. In Pittsburgh as in other cities, this area of shady business was handled by loosely organized gangs that were in constant war over turf and profits.

With the advent of Prohibition in 1923, crime exploded and became far more organized. In Pittsburgh, two crime organizations emerged from the gangs and rivalries erupted in violence as territories and increased profits from illegal booze were fought over.

The government created a perfect storm and Pittsburgh already had years of experience to take advantage of this new opportunity.

8 One Monday in July 1926

There was a red-light district in Pittsburgh well before the one I will highlight in later chapters that pops up downtown in the 1960's. Well, technically it was not Pittsburgh, it was Allegheny City, the area now known as the northside of Pittsburgh.

Allegheny City was a separate municipality until it was usurped by Pittsburgh in 1907. The lower area of Allegheny City was as raucous as any frontier town. Gambling establishments, prostitution houses and illegal bars flourished in the area now dominated by Heinz Field and PNC Park, the home of the Pittsburgh Steelers and Pirates professional sports teams.

The district, commonly referred to as the 'tenderloin' began to take root in the late 1800s and flourished during Prohibition. Officials in Pittsburgh often 'got tough' on vice when it served their political purposes, which usually culminated in running the working ladies out of their downtown locations and across the river.

During prohibition, there was plenty of business to go around and there were pocket districts in downtown on First, Second and Third Avenues from Ross Street to the Monongahela River as well as in the Hill District clustered around Colwell Street.

However, the newly crowned northside which many residents of Allegheny City were still smarting from, was the largest. An estimated twenty blocks, stretching from Canal Street along the river, up to Federal and Isabella Streets were chocked full of vice establishments.

The era of Prohibition and the roaring 20's conjures up nostalgic images of super cool clubs, ladies in flapper dresses and well-dressed men sipping on fancy cocktails and listening to jazz. In reality, those types of establishments were few and far between and reserved for the rich.

For most of working-class Pittsburghers, the speakeasy was typically a hole in the wall. It was often a dirty and grimy backroom, basement or upstairs to a legitimate business. The bordellos were most often converted small rooms or a converted house.

These were the places that Pittsburghers took their life in their hands every day and night. With the supply of booze never able to keep up with the demand of the population who were long accustomed to a stiff drink after a shift, the next drink you took could very well be your last.

Bootleggers used every possible means in acquiring alcohol for the consumers. This often consisted of the strongest moonshine available from illegal stills, bathtub gin and worse concoctions made from stolen industrial application alcohol byproducts.

The art of chemistry flourished, as bootleggers found ways to remove the harsh chemicals that the Federal Government mandated industrial manufacturers to add to the alcohol to deter its consumption. Bartenders invented new drinks often with fruit and other flavors to mask the low grade and dangerous alcohol that they were forced to serve.

The government was legally poisoning its citizens in the name of protection. By October of 1926, Pittsburgh had already counted its 63rd death that year because of alcohol and mostly due to the poisons added to alcohol supply. To put that in today's numbers and epidemic rates, Westmoreland County, today roughly the size of Pittsburgh's population in 1926, counted nearly the same number of deaths due to Opioid overdoses in 2018.

Drinks like Jamaica Ginger and Smoke began to make it into the supply. Jamaica Ginger, known on the streets as "Jake" was a patent medicine released on the market in the 19th century. It contained 70% to 80% of ethanol alcohol and prohibition agents recognized it right away as a method to flout the new prohibition laws.

To discourage drinking, the government required a different formula that altered Jamaica Ginger into a bitter and hard to drink fluid. Undaunted bootleggers and a pair of amateur chemists worked to develop an alternative adulterant that would pass the government tests for alcohol and be somewhat pleasing to drink.

Their solution was to add a plasticizer called tri-o-tolyl phosphate, which was later found to be a neurotoxin after drinkers began to lose control of their hands and feet. You could spot a Jake drinker by their walk. They would raise their feet high with their toes flopping downward onto the pavement followed by their heels.

Smoke originated in Hell's Kitchen in New York City. It was a very simple, but deadly combination of raw alcohol, often poisonous methyl alcohol made from wood, mixed with water. It was cheap at ten cents a slug.

Ironically, there was one palace in the northside district. The third floor of the Kenyon Theater on Federal Street was the one high class club. It was run by Charles Luck and another unnamed partner. It featured marble topped tables and wicker furniture. Good whiskey flowed and a highball would set you back 50 cents.

This description was available because a group of intrepid journalists invaded the district over the course of a few days and issued an amazing expose of the northside establishments. Their article blazed the front page of the Pittsburgh Post on July 26, 1926, a Monday. Their work would spark a series of reverberations and responses well into the following year though deaths would continue to rise until the eventual repeal of Prohibition in 1933.

The Kenyon Speakeasy featured a dance floor and records playing jazz or opera. On its opening night, it featured a full orchestra and a half nude dancer. The club also featured slot machines catering to the pikers who risked nickels and the plungers who risked half dollars on the games of chance.

Downstairs in the basement, Charles Faulkner ran an upscale pool hall. Inspector Faulkner was head of the Sixth Police District for the Pittsburgh Police. His district was responsible for all the northside vice district and he more than looked the other way, working to block the orders of his superiors for raids.

Not only did he run his side hustle below a speakeasy, but his police headquarters were in-between a gambling den on one side and a house of prostitution on the other. After the Post's expose, a fired-up public demanded his resignation as well as others. Faulkner would disappear for a little while on vacation to let the clamor blow over.

Raids were few and far between and usually took place to serve a purpose. Pete "The Greek" opened a gambling establishment at 34 Isabella St. He ran a dice game called barbout, which he dubbed the "fairest gambling game in the district."

Pete's establishment was raided by Faulkner's officers. Pete was arrested, but when he appeared before the magistrate, the charges were quickly dropped. It seems that Pete was not paying the "franchise fee" for running his establishment in the district. As soon as that matter was cleared up, so were his legal issues.

The infamous Garden Theater on the northside was once a swanky speakeasy

Other Well-Known Northside Establishments:

"The law of the State and the Nation stop on the North banks of the Allegheny and Ohio"

Mose Kelsch ran the Huppert Tavern at East and Milroy streets. The Post described it as filthy and in disorder. Kelsch served high test colored moonshine and featured two slot machines and six small rooms to entertain women.

Kelsch formerly ran the Cozy Corners Inn in Ross Township. His piano player put that place out of business when he shot and killed a married woman in the joint.

Edward Kane ran a gambling joint at 118 Federal Street. His wife, Stella Shaner, ran a Bordetella at 212 East Robinson Street. Their son Walter Kane worked the craps table. His wife, a local actress, caused a stir when she sued Stella for "alienating Walter's affections", which she valued at $10,000.

Prostitutes were readily available on East Lacosk Street. Rooms were available at the William F. Hotel or the Savoy Hotel.

The speakeasy at 24 Cajou Way served moonshine that was "guaranteed to kill at twenty paces". It was just 10 x 20 hole in the wall. Drinkers could head on over to the gambling joint at 222 Lacock Street, which had the same owner. Both joints were never raided.

The Bluebird Inn at 519 West Lacock Street was owned by Luther Zimmerman and catered to African Americans. It featured a piano player and a dance floor and liquor flowed freely.

The Park Hunting and Fishing Club at 4 East Stockton may have been run by a city official. It was raided several times by federal agents, but never by local cops and was never closed for very long.

The Northside was the center of vice in the city and would also give rise to organized crime, but not before it became a battleground.

9 The Wettest Building in Pittsburgh

With speakeasies booming in multiple parts of the city, a well-established vice district on the Northside and a population and police force that had a laisse faire attitude towards enforcement, the demand for booze was nearly insatiable.

Booze shipments were boldly run on the back of wagons into the city. These were easy marks for the prohibition agents, and they made sporadic displays of enforcement by apprehending a large shipment, cracking the barrels open and spilling them into the gutters leading to the rivers.

Whether this activity was inspiration or simply the motivation for invention, the rum runners began using the greatest assets of the city, its three rivers to deliver booze. The booze could easily be disguised under legitimate cargo and the river system was a transportation system with plenty of infrastructure already in place for off-loading.

The landscape around Pittsburgh was dotted with farms and wooded areas. Raw supplies were readily available for making alcohol and stills could be fairly hidden from prying eyes. This gave Pittsburgh a ready local supply of alcohol.

There were also attempts to locate stills closer to the customers. The Northside had their own still located at 112 West Park Way. It was a large distillery operating right under the noses of the city officials. It produced 1,000 gallons daily that flowed into the Northside establishments without the need of dangerous transportation.

Protection was prevalent for illegal businesses on the Northside, and the still was yet another blatant example of the corruption running wild in the district and the ignorance and ineptitude of enforcement provided by the city center across the river. The still would eventually be sacrificed in a public demonstration of enforcement to satisfy a public outcry.

The raid was a temporary inconvenience for the Northside establishments, requiring booze to be imported from the outlying areas. There were temporary shortages from time to time, but the larger establishments never went without product. The smaller establishments got creative and made small batches in basements and bathrooms of the local houses.

One of the largest area production facilities was located on the Cavanaugh Farm in Elizabeth, PA. Elizabeth sits upriver from Pittsburgh on the Monongahela. The river winds its way North from West Virginia through idyllic wooded valleys, bending its way to Pittsburgh.

The Mon Valley, as it's known, was the center of the Whiskey Rebellion, where farmers took up arms against the fledgling United States government and its scheme to raise money with a tax on whiskey, a staple of the area.

It is also the cradle of industrial production that built the nation. Steel from the mills in the valley went into Chrysler automobiles and the Golden Gate bridge. The workers that made the steel and mined the area coal fields had always enjoyed unwinding with an adult beverage.

Elizabeth was an ideal location to launch shipments into the city. Merriweather Lewis and William Clark are known to begin their journey from Pittsburgh on their famous exploration. However, they used Elizabeth as a boatbuilding and staging area, stopping in Pittsburgh to gather more supplies.

For the rum runners, the Cavanaugh Farm to Pittsburgh run was very profitable. Disguising the booze shipments with other cargo, it was a short trip into the city. Cargo was often off-loaded for Pittsburgh where Point State Park is today. However, the rum runners could stop just short of this official area, close to the Mon Wharf.

There they could quickly offload the hooch before continuing. Tunnels were created leading from the river to the basement of the building at 120 Boulevard of the Allies. Tunnels were deployed in other cities as an effective means of getting booze supplies into the cities. Tunnels were used in Los Angeles, Chicago, and the Ybor City neighborhood of Tampa.

The building at 120 Boulevard of the Allies acted as a waystation or short-term warehouse with thousands of gallons of booze passing through it. As such, even though it was not a drinking establishment, it was the wettest building in Pittsburgh.

From here, the booze could be broken down into small shipments that could be clandestinely transferred easily to the speakeasies, especially the downtown cluster around first, second and third avenues. It was also a short trip to the Northside and Hill District red-light neighborhoods.

Today, the tunnels are long gone. They were never engineered for longevity but proved to be very effective to move booze right under the noses of law enforcement. The building at 120 is often referred to as Pavilion X. It has been remodeled extensively on the inside and the prohibition evidence has been wiped away.

It is now the home of the east coast facility for the National Bioskills Laboratories. It is equipped with a 72-seat stadium-seating auditorium as well as seven surgical stations and numerous meeting areas filled with technology.

National Bioskills boasts that it is "within walking distance of riverfront parks and numerous hotels and restaurants". Those same amenities made it attractive in the age of Prohibition as well

10 The Bumpy Rise of Organized Crime

John Volpe

Two gangs would emerge to control bootlegging, gambling, and other vice in the city, but not without a bumpy and bloody consolidation over several years. The violence started in earnest well into Prohibition in 1927.

On the Northside with its long-established vice district and abundance of drinking establishments was fertile ground to establish a strong power base. In fact, the Pittsburgh family can trace its line directly to the Northside gang.

Two brothers, Stefano and Sam Monastero, would fight their way to the top and use the Northside as a base to expand their criminal organization. They owned the north and the west of the city and began to move on Downtown and the Hill District.

In the east, the Volpe Brothers controlled the booze and the politics based out of the Italian enclave of Wilmerding in the shadows of George Westinghouse's factory. They would move on the Hill District and Downtown as well.

Ignazio Volpe had sired eight strapping brothers. One short of a ball team, but plenty enough to run one of the largest bootlegging organizations in the city. His son, John Volpe, was the leader. He was charming and ruthless.

If you wanted alcohol, the Volpes had you covered, operating out of a supermarket in Wilmerding. A customer simply pulled up to the store, parked and placed their order. The Volpes would take their car and drive it to their secret location. There they would place the booze order in the trunk and return the car to the market.

The two gangs rubbed out any rivals that got in their way. The first victims were the men controlling the Hill District rackets. Luigi Lamendola, a thug, opened a speakeasy in the neighborhood and demanded the other establishments buy their booze from him. In two years-time he would be shot dead outside of his bar.

Between the Monasteros and the Volpes, the body count would continue to rise. A total of 93 murders would occur over these blood-filled years. Moonshiners that ran across the controlled territories would be lucky if they were just chased out of town. The Volpes would be successful in controlling prices and move their office into the Rome Coffee Shop in the Hill District.

The Monasteros were not so lucky in maintaining their leadership positions. In 1929, ambitious men came for them. Stefano was gunned down in front of St. John's General Hospital in the Northside. Sam survives the hit, but less than a year later, he would be found in his car with his own necktie used as a garrote.

With the Monasteros now out of the way, John Bazzano came into power atop the Northside gang that was now being recognized as an organized family. Rather than fight the Volpes, Bazzano proposed an alliance, creating a strong crime family in Pittsburgh.

In 1931, Charles "Lucky" Luciano set out to change the face of crime in the United States forever and would have a resounding impact in Pittsburgh as well. That was the year that the Commission, a ruling body, was formed uniting and regulating organized crime across the country.

Lucky created the five families of New York and gave them equal representation on the Commission along with Al Capone's Chicago Outfit and the Magaddino Family of Buffalo. The Pittsburgh family, still in its infancy, was assigned to Luciano's Family which would be later renamed the Genovese Family.

With this developing structure, Luciano recognized both John Bazzano and John Volpe as heads of criminal activity in Pittsburgh. Pittsburgh now had increased resources through New York as well as tighter oversight. However, business was booming at home, making both men rich, with little police interference.

Sure, there were the occasion raids, and the booze was confiscated, prostitutes ended up in jail overnight and low-level managers would go to jail sometimes for a little longer. In general, none of the big guys went to jail with one exception.

Federal agents set up one of the younger Volpe brothers, Louis, in a sting operation. He ended up serving more time than expected for selling an undercover agent a small amount of alcohol. If Louis was to be made an example of, it was a useless gesture as business continued unabated.

The peace created between John Bazzano and the Volpe faction of the family would be short lived. The Volpe brothers controlled some of the richest rackets and John Volpe was a threat to Bazzano's tenuous hold on the family.

In 1932, Bazzano would make a move to shore up all accounts and it would go down in as one of the most notorious days in Pittsburgh history. It was a warm Friday in July, and it would be John Volpe's last day.

The Pittsburgh Post-Gazette detailed John's last day. All in all, it wasn't that bad. It included a haircut and shave downtown and a stop for a milkshake. John then joined his brothers and other members of his crew at his Hill District headquarters in the Rome Coffee Shop.

The coffee shop was owned by a member of his crew and most days the Volpe brothers hung out playing cards with other members. This day was no different.

John Volpe stepped back outside for some reason, maybe to have a smoke. A Ford Sedan approached, stopped and three men got out. John Volpe would have recognized their leader, "Big" Mike Spinelli. Spinelli was a top Bazzano lieutenant and had worked with the Volpes. His intentions were different this day.

John Volpe must have read those intentions in his eyes or posture. He took off and ran towards where his car was parked. John Volpe had ordered a custom-made Cadillac Coupe, complete with bullet proof windows. If he could make it to the car, his life would be saved.

The gunmen opened fire. John Volpe was struck five times and fell to the curb, dead in a pool of blood. He just wasn't quick enough. The gunmen did not stop there. They entered the coffee shop and proceeded to eliminate the remaining Volpe brothers.

Inside, men scattered for safety. James Volpe was shot three times from behind. Poor Albert Volpe died in a bowl of cereal, his lunch for the day. Two gunmen left via the front door, one from the back door. All three were back in the Ford and gone before police would arrive.

John Volpe lay dying in the gutter. Reverend Eugene McGuigan was passing the scene on a streetcar. He leapt off and made his way through the gathering crowd to administer last rites to the fallen crime boss.

The massacre happened in broad daylight with hundreds of potential witnesses. The owner of the Rome Coffee Shop, Santo Bazzano, would have recognized Spinelli and possibly the two other gunmen. However, he told cops he did not know who killed the Volpes nor why anyone would have reason.

The largest manhunt in Pittsburgh history would commence - and go absolutely nowhere. Those in the neighborhood told investigators that they heard the shots but knew better than to investigate. None of Volpe's crew would finger the shooters either.

Privately, Bazzano was suspected of organizing the killings. With no witnesses, he and Spinelli would avoid arrest. Bazzano had eliminated a potential rival and the family would be united under his leadership. He was poised to head the nascent Pittsburgh organized crime family. But, not for long.

The murder of the Volpes would be one of the first tests of Luciano's Commission. One of its cardinal rules were that bosses could not be killed without the Commission's permission. John Volpe was considered a boss, Bazzano had not sought permission before his move on the faction.

A week later, Bazzano was summoned to New York City to appear before the Commission and was handed the sentence for his disobedience – capital punishment. His body was found in Brooklyn with twenty stab wounds and blood-stained handkerchief in his mouth.

Spinelli would flee the country, eventually ending up back in Italy by way of Canada. He was arrested by Italian authorities and spent thirty years in prison but avoided extradition to the United States.

About a year later, prohibition would end. Though it arguably never began in Pittsburgh. Pittsburghers did rejoice in the ability to drink in the open again. Alcohol deaths returned to normal levels as well now that dangerous chemicals added by the federal government to deter drinking and the questionable methods for purification to get around these additives were no longer necessary.

Violence also decreased in Pittsburgh. Prohibition gave rise to organized crime around the nation, and organizations were flush with cash from bootlegging to expand operations into additional lucrative enterprises and rackets.

In Pittsburgh, Bazzano's move for complete power succeeded in creating a unified Pittsburgh Family out of the competing gangs. Vincenzo Capizzi would rise to boss after Bazzano's murder. He would retire in 1937, replaced by Frank Amato, who would expand the gambling rackets.

In 1956, Amato yielded the title of boss due to illness to John Sebastian LaRocca who would lead the family for nearly thirty years through the golden age of organized crime.

11 The Queen Before the King

George Lee figures prominently in several of the Notorious Pittsburgh stories. Before he would make his rise to the throne as Pittsburgh's Vice King, Pittsburgh would have a Queen of Vice. Her name was Nettie Gordon and she ruled over the Northside Red Light District for more than twenty years.

Gordon arrives in Pittsburgh around 1900 from West Virginia. She was described as a very beautiful and shrewd businesswoman. Descriptions are the only thing we must go on as Gordon would never let her picture be taken.

Many photographers would try, but all would fail with photos of Gordon's arms covering her face or clothing shading her from the camera lens. Gordon was also very talented at evading arrest.

Gordon ran a brothel at 211 West Canal Street, just blocks away from where the sports stadiums now sit on the Northside of Pittsburgh. The red-light district stretched over many blocks and there were many players in the vice racket, but Gordon was the queen.

All other houses of ill repute answered to her as did police and politicians. In fact, Gordon was a politician herself. She was elected to the office of Republican Ward Committee Woman in the 22nd Ward.

Gordon would see Allegheny City transition to Pittsburgh and the start and end of prohibition. Through it all she would be protected by the Northside's police and politicians. The former Allegheny city residents seemed to enjoy snubbing their nose at the city's leadership across the river.

Gordon's brother was a motorcycle cop for the Pittsburgh Police and other officers showed loyalty to this relationship. Inspector Charles Faulkner, Chief of the Sixth Police District was also a supporter and protector of Gordon and her business interests.

Faulkner went out of his way for Gordon. He posted officers in front of her brothel to discourage any public officials from interfering as well as any other underworld characters that may have wanted to move into the territory.

Faulkner deliberately ignored orders for raids on Gordon. He even lobbied and sparred with his superiors to cancel planned operations. He frustrated Public Safety Director James Clark on more than one occasion as Clark sought to shutdown Gordon.

Gordon may have had the police and politicians on her side, but she did face serious opposition. In the face of lax policing of Prohibition laws in Pittsburgh, the church would rise as its most effective enforcer.

Many churches of the day used their influence in support of Prohibition. A few were the firebrands that stirred their congregation to action, bringing pressure to bear on politicians. This public outcry and the threat of lost votes was often the only effective motivation for the indifferent to corrupt city leadership to act.

The Reverend Dr. Percival H. Barker made it his personal mission to convert Gordon to more righteous ways. Barker was the minister of the Point Breeze Presbyterian Church where Director Clark happened to be a member.

Barker urged through his sermons and in private conversations for Clark to take in the 'scarlet woman', Gordon. Barker was confident if he could get Gordon into his church and even into his own house that he could show her the error of her ways.

Barker's sermon professed that the only way to eliminate vice was to "go into the houses and spread Christianity. Clark, either moved by Barker or motivated by his frustrations with Faulkner, found a way to crack Gordon's protection.

In February 1927, Clark brought in police from other districts and by running an end around Falkner, raided Gordon's place. Jackie Davis, who worked in the house, was arrested for prostitution during the raid. Gordon and Davis quarreled over $478 in wages, and now facing arrest, agreed to testify against her.

Clark secured a grand jury indictment, and the magistrate issued a warrant for arrest for Gordon. When agents showed up to take Gordon in, she charmed them. Agreeing to turn herself in to authorities at the courthouse, she was not arrested. Clark fumed.

He would be even more upset when Gordon did arrive. If Gordon was going to jail, she was going to go in style. She pulled up to the courthouse in a limousine dressed very fashionably with much pomp and circumstance.

Apparently feeling the pressures of the job, the magistrate decided to take a vacation out of town. Faulkner also left town. Clark's star witness, Davis, well she took advantage of the opportunity and disappeared as well.

The case would fall apart, and Clark and other officials would face scrutiny for the incompetence. Gordon was free and would return triumphantly to Isabella Street to continue her reign. It was politics as usual.

By the time Prohibition came to an end, Gordon was slowing down. She was struggling with several health issues. She passed away in 1934. Her funeral was fitting of her queenly status. Many turned out to see her off. It was a closed casket of course. Even in death, she did not want to be captured in a photograph.

Visitors still leave coin offerings on Gordon's grave to this day.

The Northside red-light district would eventually dry up, and blight would take over the neighborhood instead. Even with the redevelopment with the construction of the stadiums and other businesses, there are still pockets of blight today.

The red lights would move to a swankier location taking up residences on Penn and Liberty Avenues in downtown Pittsburgh.

Pittsburgh's Red-Light District Part 1

The term red-light district originates from the red lights that brothels once used as signs. Red lights did not line the buildings on Liberty and Penn Avenues in Pittsburgh, but there was a concentration of X-rated businesses.

Bookstores carried the latest porn magazines and novelties and offered peep shows in the back rooms. Above them, massage parlors bloomed as a home for prostitution. Prostitution was on the street corners as well. There were strip clubs and movie houses that went XXX.

The area wasn't there, then it suddenly was. It began to take shape in the late sixties and was in its prime throughout the seventies. Pittsburgh and its institutions would work for nearly thirty years to completely clean it up starting in the early eighties and with the help of Federal authorities.

During this brief time, some of the most notorious characters in Pittsburgh would use this adult playground setting to act out true stories that would make Hollywood proud.

12 How did the Red-Light District Come About?

"I didn't know Pittsburgh still had a red-light district," said a friend to me when I told him about the walking tour. "Well, they do, and they don't," was my reply. The fact is that the Pittsburgh Cultural Trust has done a phenomenal job in transforming the area into the cultural district with theaters, galleries and other activities in the buildings that once housed red-light businesses.

Before this area became a red-light district, it was Pittsburgh's theater district. The Benedum Center and Heinz Hall, now performing arts foundations of the cultural district, were once grand movie palaces. People flocked downtown to see the blockbuster films of the 30's, 40's and 50's.

Pittsburgh's red-light district rose almost out of nowhere in the late 1960's. Both Penn and Liberty Avenues were home to several three and four-story buildings that were available for a low investment. These buildings were perfect for a red-light business.

The street-level retail was either a legitimate business or a 'news' outlet that carried X-rated materials. This juxtaposition made for some interesting stories.

In one of the arcades that dotted the area, a young man on break in-between classes could be banging away on the pinball machines. If he takes the time to look up, a woman might roll by on her roller skates on the way to her job and clients upstairs.

A woman reminisced about going to dance classes which were in a second-floor studio above a bathhouse. She remembers asking her mother, "Why don't they take their baths at home?" Innocence among the excess.

However, it was a theater's transformation that would become the postcard for Pittsburgh's red-light district. The Harris Theater at 809 Liberty Avenue was originally called the Art Cinema and before this area became the red-light district, it showed art house pictures.

Next door to the Art Cinema was another movie house at 807 Liberty Avenue. In the 1970's, it was struggling, and made the decision to begin showing X-rated films. The Art Cinema soon followed suit. The Roman massage parlor popped up at 801 to serve the same clientele. Just that quick, the entire block became the center of the red-light district.

The methodical advance of the red-light district was the result of a few enterprising individuals that saw an opportunity to make a quick buck. It also helped that vice was well organized at the time.

Since the 1950's, vice was under the control of one-man - George Lee. Lee would eventually earn the title, 'the Vice King of Pittsburgh'. By day Lee was an iron worker. By night he rose to run all the massage parlors and an X-rated distribution operation.

Lee got his start by hosting sex parties in his Shadyside home. When you hear "sex parties" from this time, people think key parties, where women would draw a set of keys from a bowl and that would be her partner for the evening.

Lee's parties were nothing of the sort. In fact, the parties were not for 'lifestyle' couples that were looking to meet others with similar interests. Lee's parties were organized prostitution that catered to Pittsburgh's elite.

Lee would organize the girls for entertainment opportunities and his party guests would compensate him for his efforts. The *little black book* would come into play here as well. Lee kept track of his clientele and they had obvious reasons to not have these activities publicly exposed.

When Lee was asked about his black book by a reporter, he smirked, "I don't have a black book. It's green and has thousands of names in it!" That would explain how he managed to stay under the radar of the law for so long.

Another explanation for this was his connection to the Pittsburgh mafia. In an earlier story, George Lee was connected to Anthony Lagatutta as co-owners of the Court Bar. Between George and the mob, the red-light district's expansion was planned, organized, and successful.

George Lee was not what you expect from a vice lord. He would not be the prototypical character you see in movies. As mentioned earlier, Lee was an iron worker and even when he moved his business to the masses on Liberty Avenue, he kept his same dress of work boots and a work shirt, complete with a pocket protector. Not who you would picture as the premier sex peddler of Pittsburgh to be.

Lee did allow himself a few luxuries. He would trade the truck he drove to job sites for his Cadillac at night. He also traded his wife for a young working girl as well.

It is important to note that while the Pittsburgh family was likely collecting some sort of the fee or profits from the vice rackets, the major players in Pittsburgh were regulars, not major organized crime figures.

Lee found Nick DeLucia when he was a washed-up, retired firefighter moonlighting as a security guard to make ends meet for his young family. DeLucia started out as the manager of the Gemini massage parlor, Lee's flagship establishment.

George Lee

Lee also plucked Dante "Tex" Gill from the stables at Schenley Park. Gill oversaw several of Lee's massage parlors and had other managers reporting to him. Mel Cummings ran a car dealership and a strip club.

Vice in Pittsburgh would be in hands of Lee, Gill and DeLucia for many years to come with authorities trying unsuccessfully to shut them down. When Lee was asked why he was involved in the X-rated business, he replied, "What else am I going to do at night, watch TV?"

It is also important to note that these were not good guys either. To work in the massage parlors meant you were working in prostitution and in essence the parlor owners and managers were pimps, just in a more organized form.

They were tough on the women. Lee was arrested in 1972 on a complaint of assault and battery. Lorraine Ammen, 24 at the time, filed the complaint after Lee attempted to force her to commit a sexual act with him at the Gemini, where he hired her as a masseuse. She fled the parlor at 5 in the morning to "evade his advances".

Women working in the parlors were not always of age either. Morals charges, laws put in place to protect minors, would be brought frequently against Lee and others when a mother would find that her daughter was hanging around the parlors.

Pittsburgh's red-light district was open for business, and business was good. Maybe too good.

13 The Vice King is Dead

Pittsburgh was amid what typically is its coldest month, February. It was the night of the 12th. The year was 1977. The wind blows in from the rivers and down the corridor of Liberty Avenue. Nick DeLucia was hunched in his jacket, his cap pulled low on his head to stave off the cold. He was on his way to meet George Lee. Luckily it was only a few blocks from the Gemini massage parlor to Tambellini's Restaurant.

Tambellinis was a Pittsburgh institution at 139 7th Avenue. The restaurant served Pittsburgh's Italian food for more than sixty years, closing in February of 2013. It was founded by Mary Tambellini Pellegrini, her sister, Frances Tambellini D'Amico, and her uncle, Frank Tambellini, in 1950.

Proper Brick Oven and Tap Room took over the space, completely renovating the interior in the process. The exterior of the building, though, remains as it would look that 1977 cold night.

George Lee often had dinner here. He would walk down from his office at the Gemini, often in the company of a lady friend. He had taken up with Debra Dremsek and she would accompany him to dinner on this fateful night.

Lee and Dremsek would have walked through the door to a greeting and a joke from Nicholas Gazzo. Gazzo was the longtime bartender at Tambellini's. He was quick with a joke and knew your name and drink if you were a regular. Gazzo would have Lee's drink poured before he even sat down at the table.

Dremsek was no stranger to the vice rackets. In fact, she features in several of our stories and was mixed up with many of the key players. She worked in the massage parlors and was arrested for prostitution in the raid of the Spartacus Lounge in McKees Rocks.

DeLucia would join them later for after dinner drinks. DeLucia had risen to be Lee's top lieutenant. He ran the Gemini for Lee and oversaw other lower managers at other massage parlors. He knew Lee's business inside out.

Cracks, large ones, were beginning to form in Lee's empire. A week earlier, the Northside warehouse of Majestic News had been raided by the Feds. Majestic was Lee's distribution business. Although the parlors did very well and produced cash, Majestic was far more profitable.

The raid didn't only impact Lee's profits. It turned up several off-duty police officers that were moonlighting as security guards. Several were arrested, including two men that were connected to the Youngstown faction of the Cleveland mafia.

Lee had been questioned a few days before by Federal agents in Pittsburgh about his involvement with Majestic and other business ties. The Federal Government's crackdown on organized crime was in its early stages and they were looking hard for a case they could build against Stephen LaRocca, the head of the Pittsburgh family.

When the trio finally broke up at Tambellini's, Dremsek did not leave with Lee. She and DeLucia walked back up the street to the Gemini. Lee left alone headed to his Cadillac. Most nights, he parked it in the alley behind the restaurant.

The alley was, and still is, dark and shadowy. A single light dimly illuminated Lee's car. Ironically, there is still a single light in the alley, almost in perfect position for a reenactment. Lee walked down the alley from the Penn Avenue entrance.

Alley where George Lee was gunned down

Lee would not be able to see the two men approaching from the shadows at the far end of the alley. They knew his routine and were in prime position in the shadows. Lee got to his car and began fishing for his keys in his pocket.

He likely heard the men's shoes clacking against the pavement as they emerged from their hiding places and charged to make up the distance from their position to where the car was parked.

Lee was fumbling, trying to open the car door. As he got it open, he looked up and towards his attackers as they came into the light. Their guns were raised. The men did not hesitate. They opened fire. Pop, pop, pop, pop. 4 shots hit Lee in the shoulder, the chest, and the hip.

Lee slumped next to the open card door. The men did not stick around. An escape route was planned as efficiently as the hit was. The men ran down Seventh Avenue and across the bridge. There on the Northside, a pickup car was waiting. They were gone before the police sirens sounded. A pool of blood was already gathering under Lee.

The newspaper headlines screamed the next day that the Vice King was dead. The sensational story was on everyone's lips. The city reacted by trying to close Lee's businesses, but they quickly passed into the hands of DeLucia, Dante "Tex" Gill and Mel Cummings.

Lee on the other hand sat in cold storage for several months. His estate was a mess and did not even have enough assets to bury him. All the illicit income that he earned just disappeared into the ether.

It was obvious to the investigators that this was a professional hit. It was well planned and executed. Rumors around town speculated that Lee in his discussion with the Feds had made a deal that would keep him out of jail.

Pittsburgh and Cleveland were amid a turf war centered around which family would control Youngstown and its lucrative labor rackets. The raid on Majestic turned up two members from Cleveland. The question was, had Lee make a deal with the rival group?

Either of those actions would be enough to make LaRocca nervous. Add into the lethal mix, an ambitious underling with designs on the empire in DeLucia with his own ties to the family.

To this day, no one was ever arrested for Lee's murder. There were suspicions, but many leads lead to dead ends – one of them literally. Anthony "Nino" Siciliano was scheduled to stand trial for the murder of Bobby Pugh, a massage parlor manager.

Debra Dremsek was with Pugh's wife, Valerie, the night he was murdered. Pugh's body was found at a Scott Twp. address with Dremsek's name on the mailbox. Pugh worked for Gill and may have been caught up in the fight for control of the parlor business.

Siciliano was a foot soldier in the Pittsburgh mafia and the brother-in-law of DeLucia. Siciliano was charged with Pugh's murder. Right before it was scheduled to go to trial, he proclaimed that he was "ready to open up about the massage parlor killings". The plural, killings, is what interested investigators. Did he know who killed Lee?

Unfortunately, Siciliano ended up in Passavant Hospital in the North Hills in a coma. His wife had called emergency services, reporting that her husband had some sort of an attack. A drug overdose was suspected. He died ten days later at the age of 31.

The cause of death was listed after an autopsy as "active disease processes", but his death was a mystery. Accusations swirled that he was poisoned or that the drug overdose was forced swirled. The trial, less than a month away, was cancelled. No other suspects emerged in Lee or Pugh's death and DeLucia was never connected to either.

One thing was certain though, with Lee out of the way, a war for control of the massage parlors heated up between Lee's lieutenants, and it was about to get bloody.

14 **The Stage is Set**

The 900 block of Liberty Avenue would be the last block in the red-light district to give up. The block was filled with dilapidated nuisance bars. Chief among them was the Stage, a strip club that had seen better days.

The city's Urban Redevelopment Authority worked to get control of these buildings any way possible and chose to level the whole block to make way for the construction of the August Wilson Center that celebrates the Pittsburgh born playwright.

The Stage strip club was at 966 Liberty Avenue. It was managed for George Lee by Mel Cummings. Cummings was not your prototypical strip club manager. He was 5'10" but portly with big glasses, a beard and shaggy hair. He worked at the Auto Palace car dealership, and the Stage, well it seemed like a creative outlet for him.

Cummings met Lee when he came into buy a car. He claimed to have known him for 25 years, seeing him socially and even fishing in Florida together. He was interviewed after Lee's death but stated he did not know who killed his friend, though that he was sure it was not organized crime.

Cummings believed he was an innovator and marketing genius. The club was only featuring women dancers at the time. Cummings decided he could increase business if he added male dancers as well.

In the seventies, his male dancers were shirtless with tight gold shorts. The women at that time were not fully nude as well due to the current ordinances. All the dancers were young, and Cummings lorded over the place from a seat at the bar.

Upon Lee's assassination, the massage parlors were distributed by Lee's lawyer to his lieutenants. Three, including the Gemini flagship, went to Nick DeLucia. Three others, including the Spartan in McKees Rocks went to Dante "Tex" Gill. The Stage was given to Cummings.

This arrangement did not make DeLucia happy. After Lee's death, he felt he should have control over the entire X-rated empire. Legally, he did not have much recourse unless the other owners would take a buyout offer.

DeLucia went to see Cummings first, offering to buy the Stage. Cummings and Lee had a relationship before DeLucia joined the organization. Cummings viewed himself as the reason the Stage was successful and did not wish to take the offer.

Cummings became more nervous after Lee's death. He gave an interview that claimed he was "living in bull's-eye". He put on 35 pounds from nervous eating, and chain smoked three packs a day. He also started taking different routes from work to home to not have a pattern.

DeLucia had a bigger fish to deal with in Gill. He had to get Cummings to sell to put pressure on Gill. DeLucia didn't think Cummings would stand in his way and now something had to be done.

The next day, Cummings was returning to his apartment in the Hill District from his work at the Oakland dealership. He drove a green Lincoln Continental that he kept immaculate. The car had all the latest upgrades.

Cummings parked in the complex's private parking facility in the back. He pulled into the lot and drove to his designated spot which was at the far end. Little did he know that there was a sniper waiting in the bushes.

Cummings rounded the car into the parking spot as shots rang out from the bushes. The barrage sprayed the car, shattering the glass on the driver's side door and windshield. A shot hit the steering wheel, and another hit the head rest. However, by some miracle, Cummings was only struck in the shoulder.

The Continental saved Cummings life. A metal rod in the head rest was strong enough to deflect a bullet that would have struck him in the neck, liking killing him. Investigators found the high-powered rifle nearby but were unable to trace it.

Only one arrest was made, and it was Cummings, himself. He was indicted when police found a gun in his car. Cummings had been convicted in Texas on gambling charges in 1971. Cummings had bought the gun for protection after Lee was gunned down.

Cummings would recover and attempt to hold onto the Stage. Shortly after the attempted hit though, DeLucia Enterprises had acquired the property, surprisingly in an alliance with Gill. Cummings unsuccessfully fought the transfer in court, and gradually fades into retirement from the rackets.

The partnership between DeLucia and Gill would not last long.

Pittsburgh's Red-Light District Part 2

1977 would be a defining year for vice in Pittsburgh. It began with Lee's death, and it would go out with a bang, literally. The struggle for control did not end that year, but this first year of the war was its bloodiest.

In just three short years after, it would all unravel as the city and its residents would finally have enough. The demand for services would not go away, but the method of delivery would begin to change.

However, before the red light is turned off, there are still several more notorious stores to share.

15 The Christmas Bombing

It was unseasonably warm on December 23, 1977. Unusual for Pittsburgh but enjoyed none the less. Liberty Avenue was bustling with the season. Cars filled the street on their way to or from the city, many filled with treasures found in the downtown department stores.

Imagine those shoppers as they were making their way up and down the sidewalks, on their way back to their cars or off to another store. There were three major department stores in Pittsburgh at the time which are now long-gone Kaufman's, Gimbel Brothers and Joseph Horne's Department Store were destinations at this time of year.

The stores were brightly decorated with window displays. Horne's had a huge tree on the corner of the store. This is still lit during the holidays today – one of the few remnants of a storied retail past. However, for a kid at the time, the big draw was the rooms full of toys. Some that you didn't even imagine existed and hoped that Santa Claus might put under your tree.

Horne's was on Stanwix Street between Penn and Liberty. Kids and their parents crowded the sidewalks around the area as they did some last-minute shopping or dreaming for what Christmas might look like in just two days.

The streets were crammed with men and women celebrating as well. For many of the downtown office workers this was the last day before their Christmas break. Many parties were in full swing this afternoon in the office buildings that lined Liberty.

In Pittsburgh, when you get an unexpected warm day, you take full advantage of it. So, the parties inevitably ended up spilling out to the sidewalks. The men rolled up their short sleeves and, with drinks in hand, continued the revelry.

At 641 Liberty Avenue, the Gemini massage parlor was quiet. There was not much business this afternoon right before Christmas. The women were having a Christmas party of their own. They were sitting in the reception lounge by the front windows. They were chatting amongst themselves occasionally glancing down to the bustle below.

In the small group was Sasha Scott. The Gemini supposedly had the prettiest women out of any parlor. None was in more demand than Sasha. She was the draw at the Gemini, the top grossing parlor in the city. Men fantasized about her and she, in-turn, brought their fantasies to life. Sasha was beautiful with long chestnut hair and green eyes that could seduce any beast. She was slender built with a crooked smile. Sasha was also known to be submissive and purportedly performed just about any sex act that was desired.

Sasha did not have an easy life. She may have entered prostitution as young as fifteen. From a young age, she bounced from man to man in abusive relationships. Many of these men acted as her pimp. Eventually, she ended up in the massage parlors. The Gemini was Pittsburgh's flagship, managed at this time by Nick DeLucia.

At the age of 24, Sasha married an older man by the name of Glenn Scott. Glenn was, for lack of a better term, an entrepreneur. He hustled to make ends meet and most oftentimes his business deals would be considered in the gray area. He was described as "not a bad guy, but not a good guy either".

The couple moved to the suburb of Scott Township, just south of the city, to start their life together. It would be short-lived. The couple consorted with the lower rungs of Pittsburgh's vice players. All were hungry to move up in the ranks.

Glenn continued his questionable business dealings. Another individual, Richard Henkel was moving around the vice circles at the time. Henkel was perfecting his insurance fraud scams and was getting good at them.

Henkel was not as sophisticated as a criminal when he first began. He ended up in jail in 1970 for robbery after getting away with $80,000 from a Mt. Washington bank. His partner in the crime, Lawrence Winsor, was never found. Authorities suspected that Henkel killed him to keep all the money.

Despite being handed a twenty-year sentence and sent to Federal prison in Atlanta and then Marion, IN., Henkel would be paroled after serving only three. He was described as a "model of rehabilitation".

Henkel was a fast learner, however, and he graduated from the penitentiary with new skills, including bomb-making. After trying out these new skills in ransom schemes in Ohio, Henkel was ready for the big time and a return to his Pittsburgh home.

Henkel a began enacting the insurance scams, enlisting Glenn Scott, and bodies began piling up. Though the insurance claims often paid Henkel or his mom, he was not arrested for these crimes. Glenn did not fare well as Henkel's partner. He was found shot in his apartment in Scott Twp.

With her husband and several other associates dead, Sasha remained in the life she knew. She continued to be the star attraction at the Gemini, earning her living. It is possible that she may have benefitted from the insurance policies and at least had knowledge of some of Henkel's schemes. This would be a dangerous position to be in.

Whether for benefit or naivety, Sasha was involved with Henkel. She had her own insurance policy set to pay Henkel's mom if she died.

While Pittsburgh was enjoying their pre-Christmas revelry, a plan was being put in place at Pittsburgh's Airport. Outside of a hotel at the airport, a man with a wig and fake moustache flagged a cab driver down. The man asked the cabbie to do him a special favor. He wanted to deliver a gift to his girl, but he wanted it to be a surprise

He offered the cabbie $50 to make the special delivery. All he had to do was drive it to the city and deliver it to Sasha Scott. She works at the Gemini Massage Parlor, the man explained. The cabbie knew it well and $50 was far more than a fare would pay in 1977.

The cab driver agreed, and the man gave him a brightly wrapped Christmas present with a big bow. He told the driver to make sure it was delivered straight and only to Sasha.

The cabbie sped away from the airport, wasting no time. He drove through the tunnel and into downtown. He parked his car right on the street in front of the Gemini. Following instructions, he ran the package up the steps to the massage parlor and asked for Sasha.

The women were still sitting around the front window. Sasha took the present and thanked the driver as he left. She brought the present over to where the other women were sitting. They immediately urged her to open it, curious of the mysterious gift from a romantic admirer.

Sasha relented. She began to unwrap the present, pulling on the ribbon as she did. BOOM! An explosion rocked the building. Glass blew out onto the sidewalk below, covering the shoppers and revelers. Cars stopped at the street and sirens wailed.

A fireman was first on the scene. Smoke was pouring out of the upstairs windows. He mounted the stairs to get to the second floor where he encountered dazed and confused workers and clients hurriedly descending and coughing from the smoke and debris. Some were bloodied because of the explosion. He helped them out to the street to await paramedics.

When the fireman finally reached the second floor, he found a grisly scene. Sasha was dead. The bomb had decapitated her. Miraculously, she was the only death from the bomb. The other women escaped with cuts and bruises, and many were in shock from what had just take place. However, they lived to tell the story of the "Christmas Bombing".

The bombing of the Gemini was big news over the holidays. A public outcry erupted as a result, demanding that something be done. Just a month after a contentious election, Mayor Richard Caliguiri would face his first real test in his first full term.

Caliguiri responded to the public pressure by closing all the massage parlors throughout the city. Police blazed tape across the doors and stapled the decree on the doors. The parlors were closed by order of the city.

They stayed closed for all of three days. The parlor owners retained great attorneys. The lawyers were in court as soon as possible and won a stay on the order quickly. The parlors were back open to business before the new year rang.

The police did not have much to go on. The cab driver's description did not provide any leads. He even admitted that it was obvious that the man was wearing a wig. Apparently, he did not question it at the time. An investigation of the hotel and its records turned up nothing as well. The man had never checked into a room.

Even without any hard evidence, the police still suspected Henkel. The insurance policies on both Glenn and Sasha and another massage parlor manager, Bobby Pugh, were all red flags. All three were now dead and in mysterious fashion. Yet, they were unable to connect the crimes or charge Henkel.

Debbie Dremsek, George Lee's former girlfriend, surfaced in the investigations as well. There were no hard ties to Henkel, or the crimes and she may have simply just been friends with her former colleagues. However, after the bombing and the subsequent investigation, it appears that she may have given up the life. Her name once so prominently attached to the major players in the vice racket, disappears from the newspapers.

The owner and manager of the Gemini, Nick DeLucia, was conspicuously absent from most of the stories on the bombing. The Gemini was his flagship and Sasha was his best attraction. Sasha was now gone for good, and the Gemini required massive repairs and would remain closed for some time.

Many questions arise from this situation. DeLucia had a rather large insurance policy on the Gemini and received significant compensation. Was he in on Henkel's plan? Was he a partner?

If not, this was a bold and public step for Henkel. The vice rackets, which the massage parlors were a big part of, were loosely controlled by the Pittsburgh family at the time. Unless Henkel had his own arrangements, he did not just cross a dangerous line – he leaped it in grand fashion that would not be overlooked.

The Gemini was back in business in a few short months. The public moved on to their next distraction. The authorities, however, were taking notice. With a high-profile murder of a vice boss and the Christmas Bombing, they began to step up investigations of the vice rackets in Pittsburgh, looking for connections to the mob in the process with the formation of a special task force.

16 A Hot August Night

Summer in Pittsburgh. It is either raining or it is about to rain. That cycle creates high humidity that can sometimes drive you insane. They call them dog days of August for a reason. The cycle seems to drag on before what typically is a nice September and the beginning of Autumn.

In 1978, Nick DeLucia had not quite made it to relief. It was August 29th, and it was a hot day that turned into a hot and sticky Pittsburgh night. DeLucia sat in the oppressive heat in his offices in the Mayan Health Club at 25 Market Square.

The Mayan Health Club was no gym. In fact, it was an office for the Pittsburgh family of La Cosa Nostra. The Mayan was up the stairs of 25 Market Square on the second floor. At this time in its history, it sometimes served as a massage parlor, but DeLucia had chosen to move his office to this location after the Gemini exploded in the Christmas bombing fiasco.

The Mayan overlooked Market Square. Forbes Avenue bisected the square and you could drive down the middle. It wouldn't be until a renovation in the 2000's that the road would be diverted, and a true square would be made complete with the traffic out of the middle replaced with markets and concerts.

DeLucia had not gained much ground in his empire building efforts. 1977 had been a bloody year for Pittsburgh and months of frustration for DeLucia as he sought to ascend to be the next Vice King of Pittsburgh.

George Lee was dead, and the authorities had not solved the crime. DeLucia was successful in gaining control of three of the massage parlors and had wrestled the Stage strip club away from Mel Cummings.

Dante "Tex" Gill remained in control of three of the massage parlors. DeLucia had failed to intimidate Gill and was locked in a fierce battle to take over Gill's operation. Bobby Pugh, one of Gill's parlor managers had been collateral damage.

To make matters worse, Richard Henkel had blown up the Gemini, DeLucia's flagship operation. Sasha Scott, one of his top money earners was dead. You could say that DeLucia was further behind than when he started after Lee's death.

It was well after midnight, and Market Square was empty. The businesspeople had long left for the day and the restaurants had closed several hours earlier. Downtown Pittsburgh was not a late-night city and the only thing still bustling would have been the massage parlors on Liberty and Penn Avenues several blocks away.

DeLucia's offices were on the second floor of this building in Market Square

DeLucia sat alone in his office surrounded by an arsenal. He had guns of all sorts and sizes, including semi-automatic weapons that were difficult to acquire. He had plenty of ammunition as well, enough for a small army.

The question is what was bothering DeLucia so great that he would arm himself to the teeth. Was he preparing for the next battle with Gill? Was he seeking revenge against Henkel? Perhaps, there was another threat developing.

Whether it was the heat, frustration, or some other reason, DeLucia tore down the stairs and out the door into the street. He had a semi-automatic weapon in each hand. Pointing them at the night sky, he began to unload, disturbing the silence.

A police officer a few blocks away heard the gunshots. He quickly made his way to the square. DeLucia was standing there breathing hard and covered in sweat. The officer knew DeLucia by reputation.

"Nick, what in the hell are you doing," he asked. Nick did not have an answer. The officer gave him a warning, and both went about their business.

There was much speculation for why DeLucia was stocking up. The Hollywood story would pit him against Henkel in a showdown. It would be right out of the old west, pistols at dawn in the square.

Henkel was still on the loose. He may have been working for the Pittsburgh Family as a contract killer. The head of the family, John LaRocca purportedly asked Henkel, "what will it take for you to not touch me." Henkel was certainly dangerous.

Even though Anthony Siciliano was arrested for Pugh's murder, Henkel may have actually been the murderer. Investigators believed Pugh was killed because of DeLucia's war on Gill. However, Pugh also hung around with Debra Dremsek and Sasha and Glenn Scott. All three were mixed up in Henkel's insurance fraud scheme and that may have led to Pugh's murder as well.

Henkel was certainly a wild card and likely a nuisance for DeLucia and that scenario would make a great movie ending. However, the more plausible explanation was that DeLucia was more concerned with Gill at the time.

DeLucia would continue his fight with Gill. However, his time was limited and so was the red-light district.

17 The Toughest, Sweetest Person You Ever Met

Dante "Tex" Gill

One man stood in the way of Nick DeLucia's planned empire – Dante "Tex" Gill. Gill was not someone that would easily back down.

Dante "Tex" Gill was born Lois Jean Gill. Way before gender identity was even a thought, Gill was a strong presence that even gained a modicum of acceptance in conservative Pittsburgh that is still celebrated today.

At the time, newspapers struggled to find the right pronoun for Gill, always using Ms., and describing him as a woman that prefers to dress or represent as a man. Gill is still in the papers today, as Hollywood is interested in his story. One reporter made the mistake of referring to him as her and was promptly corrected. It shows you that we have come far in Pittsburgh, and likely have Gill to thank for some of that progress.

Before, he chose to become Dante Gill, Gill worked at the stables at Schenley Park. Even though he went by Lois, he began exploring his identity by cutting his hair short and covering with a big cowboy hat. The hat would become a trademark for his look, earning him the nickname Tex.

Gill seemed to be at home at the stables, working as a blacksmith and giving riding lessons to kids and adults. Gill's toughness was established during this period, when a horse would act up while he was shoeing it, Gill would smack it on its backside to settle it down.

Young cousins that were brought to Gill for riding lessons recalled upon his death that they feared acting up in his presence. However, Gill had a very soft side and those that took lessons noticed it in the way he worked with them and the horses.

Though Gill knew the "bad" crowd in Pittsburgh and likely mingled socially with a few shady characters, he did not enter a life of crime lightly. Gill only went to George Lee for a job in the massage parlors, because he needed money while caring for his ailing mother, Agnes. Agnes died in 1973 of cancer.

Around the same time Gill made the transition to Dante, wearing men's suit and ties and that iconic cowboy hat. Gill worked out well for Lee. He was a shrewd businessperson and the working women both admired and respected him.

There were never any accusations against Gill for assault on the women that worked for him. In fact, many reported that Gill looked after them, giving them gifts and even helping them with housing. He was strict though and constantly worried about the women stealing from the establishments – so much so that he employed lie detector tests.

Gill ran off to Hawaii in the mid-seventies and married Cynthia Bruno. In 1979, Bruno petitioned to change her last name to Gill, as she was living with him as his wife. The couple eschewed publicity, but a photographer caught them walking hand in hand on Liberty Avenue with the X-rated businesses in the background.

After Lee was assassinated, to DeLucia's chagrin, Gill inherited several of the massage parlors. He not only successful expanded those businesses, but also opened new businesses across the area. Gill ran a string of businesses, including the Spartacus Massage Parlor in McKees Rocks, the Japanese Meditation Temple and the Taurean Sports Models massage parlor.

The best story to illustrate Gill's juxtaposition of sweet and tough character took place in 1978 at the Spartacus massage parlor in McKee's Rocks. Authorities were cracking down after the Gemini bombing, conducting raids on parlors to harass them out of business. It didn't work as lawyers for both DeLucia, and Gill were good at getting them reopened within days.

The Pennsylvania State Police decided to conduct a raid on the Spartacus, one of Gill's establishments. Gill was at the parlor that day. He was throwing a birthday party complete with a cake.

When the police burst in, Gill picked up the birthday cake and promptly smashed it into Pennsylvania State Trooper Gerald Fielder's face. Though the event was amusing, Gill was charged with disorderly conduct for the incident and had to pay a fine. Prostitution charges were dropped for insufficient evidence.

Incidentally, Debbie Dremsek was working for Gill at the Spartacus at the time and was arrested for prostitution during the raid. Dremsek always seemed to be in the right place at the wrong times for the notorious red-light events.

Gill vs DeLucia

DeLucia expected Gill to work for him now that Lee was gone. And they did team up to run Mel Cummings out of the Stage. However, Gill had no intention in giving up the parlors that he had gained. Nick attempted to buy Gill with no luck.

DeLucia decided to use the same tactic he used on Mel Cummings. He would hire a contract killer to take Gill out. DeLucia found George Bastian, a convicted con man that was out on bail – paid by DeLucia.

DeLucia provided Bastian with a gun and had offered him a piece of the action from the massage parlors that DeLucia stand to gain. Before the plan could be carried out, DeLucia was arrested on conspiracy charges. It seems Bastian started talking to the police and spilled the beans about the plot.

At the same time DeLucia was sitting in jail waiting to make bail, Gill was in court answering to the charges because of the Spartacus raid. Police were also investigating several bomb threats that had been called on each other's parlors. Could that have been Richard Henkel stirring up trouble or just a ruse to throw off the investigators?

Henkel was the wild card using the conflict between DeLucia and Gill for control of the rackets. He used the situation as a veil to carry out his bloody crimes. Because of DeLucia's proclivity to violence and actions, investigators were convinced that the murders happening from the Gemini's bombing to the murder of massage parlor manager, Bobby Pugh, were part of a war for control. Because of this they completely missed Henkel as a suspect.

The missing piece in the war theory was the fact that Gill or any of his associates never performed a violent act in revenge or as an offensive against Gill. If this was indeed a war, then Gill should have been a suspect in the Gemini bombing, as this was DeLucia's flagship parlor.

DeLucia and Gill seemed to be concerned about Henkel, or if they did not know it was him, the threat that was apparent. They closed their parlors at different times voluntarily after the Gemini bombing.

DeLucia wasn't done. After the unsuccessful attempt on Gill's life, he decided to go after Gill's business. Just around the corner from the Gemini, Gill had a successful parlor on Penn Avenue called the Taurean Sports Models.

On an early 1980 morning, the Taurean was firebombed. The parlor was closed, and the women and clients were all gone for the night. Gill was not there either. However, the building was not empty. On the fourth floor, there was an apartment shared by three migrant workers. All three perished in the fire that consumed the building, while they were sleeping.

Gill outlasted DeLucia. He was indicted by a grand jury in 1981 on tax evasion charges and was sent to prison. Time was running out for Gill too.

Gill vs The United States

The troubles with federal authorities escalated in 1979. DeLucia was already under investigation and scrutiny of the vice rackets was high with the hopes of also proving ties to organized crime.

Gill, meanwhile, was in the process of starting a new business, Escorts Plus. He had set up operations with a partner amongst legitimate businesses in the venerable Union Trust Building in Downtown Pittsburgh.

An undercover vice control detective answered an ad for the fledgling business that offered companions for all occasions. The ad claimed to come to your door and that senior citizens, veterans and even invalids were welcome.

The agent ordered a call to a South Hills Motel. A woman showed up within an hour. She asked for $70 for the escort call and $70 for "servicing". When she disrobed, she was arrested for prostitution.

Police came calling to Escorts Plus offices and promptly arrested Gill and others on prostitution charges. Before the charges were dropped for insufficient evidence, authorities secured search warrants for Gill's home and businesses.

One of those businesses, Take Me Paint Me, was the business that Gill claimed provided his income. It sold unpainted ceramic pieces such as wall plaques and religious statuettes out of a poorly marked storefront in the back of the old Duquesne Brewery warehouse in the Southside. It was difficult to get to and residents in the area said they rarely saw customers.

During the search, investigators seized financial and other documents related to the massage parlor and escorts business. These would become the vital evidence against Gill in a tax evasion case.

In 1984 those charges came down and thrust Gill into the media spotlight in Pittsburgh. Gill was arrested along with several others, including his estranged wife. Apparently, Bruno-Gill had become fed up with the shenanigans of her husband and had left for Texas.

The indictment claimed Gill did not report $49,000 in personal income and that two of his massage parlors failed to report $232,00 in income for the years 1977-1978. In addition, Gill was charged with collecting withholding taxes for his employees, but never paid them. Defense would claim them as independent contractors.

As the trial was beginning, everything about Gill was scrutinized by the media from his dress and appearance to his alleged involvement in prostitution. Potential jurors were asked their views on sexual activity between unmarried individuals, whether they have ever been audited by the IRS, and if the fact that Gill is a woman that dresses like a man would prejudice them. Gill was in the courtroom dressed in a light color suit and tie. Surprisingly enough, jurors showed more negativity towards prostitution than Gill's appearance.

Gill was 59 at the time. The other sensational item int the story - Bruno-Gill was returned from Texas, and also standing trial. She was 28 and there was much speculation on their relationship and partnership in the vice businesses.

Gill's defense made every effort to strike prostitution testimony from the trial. They argued that Gill was on trial for not paying taxes not what his businesses may or may not be engaged in. Whether that swayed the jury or not, they convicted Gill on the tax evasion charges anyway.

Gill was sent to Washington County prison to await sentencing. He was held in the women's section. Bruno-Gill was convicted of lesser charges and was released on probation. During sentencing, Gill's lawyers asked he be placed in a federal prison with medical facilities. Apparently, Gill had suffered a heart attack while in county lock up.

Gill was given a sentence of 13 years in the federal prison in Lexington, KY. The judge also offered a deal if Gill would close the massage parlors. Gill did so and the sentence was reduced to 7 years.

In November of 1987, Gill was released back to Pittsburgh after serving 3 years. The United States was not done with Gill. They sued him in civil court for $12.5 millions of estimated nonpaid taxes in 1991. Gill said they can ask all they want, but they are not going to get anything as he was flat broke.

The 1984 trial cemented Gill as a celebrity. The same year the Pittsburgh Press awarded Gill both the "Dubious Man of the Year" and "Dubious Woman of the Year" title. "In Tex we see the perfect symbol for the upscale androgyny of the 1980s," read the Press. "She embodies business savvy, sexual confusion and an eye for fashion like no one since Michael Jackson."

After his release from prison, Gill lived a quiet life despite being well known in Pittsburgh. He passed away in 2003 at the age of 72.

Gill's longtime lawyer, Carl Janavitz eulogized Gill as such, "She was a very good businesswoman, but she just had a different lifestyle. You're talking about a person who was very complex. She was very tough. A lot of fun. She drank a lot. She partied a lot. She could recite poetry endlessly. Irish poetry."

18 Turning Off the Red Light

Extinguishing the red light was not an easy task. In fact, the task would not completely come to an end until some thirty years later, well after all the X-rated businesses had long since moved to other locations.

The work began in earnest in the early eighties. The Heinz Endowments, a large family philanthropy created by the Heinz family known for making ketchup, began making planned investments in restoring the city's cultural assets.

The Endowments were joined by other large funding partners. From these efforts a new entity, the Pittsburgh Cultural Trust, was formed to spearhead redevelopment of the red-light district and reinvent the cultural offerings of the city.

It would prove challenging. Pittsburgh was deep in decline with steel industry, its largest employer, closing mill after mill. This brought about significant outward migration as people left the area in search of jobs to support their families. Young people left in droves to major metropolitan locations.

As hard as the times were, this economic downturn may have inadvertently helped the Cultural Trust in some way. The workers of Pittsburgh were some of the best customers of the X-rated bookstores and the services of the massage parlors. With more and more of them leaving, business in the red-light district began to decline as well.

Outwardly, the public knows the Cultural Trust as the organization that brings performances, art, cinema, festivals, and other cultural activities to Pittsburgh. In reality the Cultural Trust is one of the city's largest real estate owners and developers.

With the foundations' support, the Cultural Trust worked to acquire many of the buildings that were former red-light district businesses. The organization then renovated and rented these buildings to local arts organizations and private businesses as well. The revenue generated from real estate supports the cultural programming as well as the general operating needs of the organization.

A prime example of this activity and representation of the long process of redevelopment of the district is the former Aardvark Massage Parlor at 941 Liberty Avenue. The 900 block of Liberty Avenue was infamous for its nuisance bars and X-rated pursuits.

The Aardvark, now in the hands of the Cultural Trust, stood empty for many years waiting on a new tenant and profitable reuse. When I began giving walking tours in 2016, you could still see the faded-out letters advertising the second-floor massage parlor.

Today, the letters on the second floor advertise a new pursuit, the Arcade Comedy Theatre. The Cultural Trust renovated the building for the comedy troop. The building now houses a small theater on the ground floor and second floor performance space and lounge. The Arcade kept and framed some of the old photos of the massage parlor and they are hanging in the lounge.

The Cultural Trust also had help from the city. The Urban Redevelopment Authority acquired the decrepit bars on the other side of the street from the Aardvark. It demolished the structures, including Mel Cummings' beloved Stage to make way for the August Wilson Center.

The Cultural Trust, Pittsburgh's Foundation and the City government groups were the defining force in transforming the red-light district into the cultural district, but they were not the only force. In fact, the perfect storm would occur bringing together criminal prosecution, a change in economy and investment in redevelopment.

As the Cultural Trust was just coming together in the early eighties, the two major players in the vice rackets would end up in jail. The Internal Revenue Service would bring down Dante "Tex" Gill.

Nick DeLucia would soon follow. The IRS was building its case against him at the same time they were looking into Gill. DeLucia was arrested for tax evasion and spent considerably more time in jail than Gill.

When DeLucia emerged from jail in late eighties, his beloved vice empire was gone, and the Pittsburgh Family was significantly weaker. DeLucia would die in 1995 at the age of 75, never fully realizing the success of his predecessor and mentor, George Lee.

Vice was not fully crushed in Pittsburgh. It was run out of downtown, but it did not go away. The X-rated businesses, including the stores and massage parlors would set down new roots in the suburbs where rents were lower and police scrutiny less intense. They would not congregate in a red-light district again but radiated out to serve their clientele.

The Pittsburgh Family would undergo significant changes at this time as well. John LaRocca, who led the organization through the golden years of organized crime, had successfully held onto power for thirty years. He passed away from natural causes in 1984.

In addition to LaRocca, his two top lieutenants, Carmine "Jo Jo" Pecora and Kelly Mannerino also died in the early part of the decade. The three leaders had built a profitable enterprise and were respected nationally by the crime syndicate.

The Family leadership passed to Michael Genovese and would continue its stability until 1990. Nationwide, enforcements efforts had intensified against organized crime and Pittsburgh would not avoid the extra scrutiny.

The Federal Government had finally figured out how to use the RICO, commonly referred to as the RICO Act. RICO had been conceived twenty years earlier, but the Feds had not figured out how to use it until the landmark Commission Trial in 1985.

RICO brought down the heads of the Five Families of New York so effectively with long sentences handed out that it had an unanticipated effect of unravelling the Omerta Code of silence held sacred amongst crime family members. A slew of high-ranking organized crime officials was doing the unthinkable, testifying against their associates on behalf of the government.

In Pittsburgh, two of Genovese's bosses, Charles Porter and Louis Raucci, would become ensnarled thanks to RICO. Both were found to oversee a large narcotic trafficking ring and would face very long prison terms if convicted.

Porter decided to cooperate the authorities. His testimony would decimate the Family and even bring down associates from other organizations across the country. With organized crime in disarray and facing attacks from outside and inside forces, the Pittsburgh Family, which reported to the Genovese Family in New York, was instructed to not induct any new members.

With the flow of new leadership halted, the Pittsburgh Family began a new fight for survival – one against attrition. The vice rackets were never as lucrative as other criminal activities and often invited more trouble than they were worth. As such, the largest financier of the red-light district had also left the scene.

On final major change happened in the eighties, the invention of the VCR. This would be a significant business model change and supported the move of business to the suburbs. Porn had moved to the home, and it made sense to be closer to better serve this clientele.

The perfect storm was complete. Pittsburgh's economic decline and other market forces shifted the X-rated business to the suburbs. The major vice players were in jail or gone and the Pittsburgh Family had its attentions drawn elsewhere. The Cultural Trust had a mission and resources to grab the real estate and develop it to new uses.

The red lights would go out all through the district and Pittsburgh would again have its Cultural District. This reincarnation would grow bigger and stronger with significant resources to support it. Today it is a huge economic contributor to the region, and it draws tourists from around the world.

You can still partake of vice on Liberty Avenue. It just isn't as outwardly marketed as before. You must look a little harder and take more risks, but vice is still there.

And it likely will be there forever. It is, after all, named Liberty Avenue.

Some of My Other Favorite Notorious Stories

I could not end this book without telling a few of my other favorite notorious stories of Pittsburgh. Mike Kalina's is heartbreaking and has been a part of my walking tours. Richard Henkel's story weaves through the red-light district, but it neither started nor ended there.

While doing research for other stories, I came across some interesting characters and stories. By including them at the end of the book, they bring a fitting end to organized crime in Pittsburgh that began in earlier chapters. I even looked into my crystal ball to see into the potential future notorious event. Though it is a work of fiction, I attempted to root it into what could be a plausible near future happening.

There is one common theme to these stories. Each one features a heavy dose of ambition, and it went unchecked. Boundaries are pushed. Morals can be questioned. Some end in flames.

19 The Serial Killer That Most Pittsburgher's Don't Know

With the rise in intertest in true crime, many serial killers are now household names either by their given name or the nickname assigned to them. It is odd then that Pittsburgh does not readily recall the name of one of its most lethal serial killers – Richard Henkel.

When we first met Henkel in this book, he had just blown-up Sasha Scott and the Gemini massage parlor. Earlier he had shot and killed Glenn Scott, Sasha's husband. He collected on both of their insurance policies and avoided arrest.

Henkel wasn't always a master criminal. In fact, in many ways, he was a bumbling criminal, pulling off schemes only to be easily caught. But he did share one of the most common qualities with other serial killers. He was charismatic, charming, and convincing. He would hone this over time.

Henkel made a huge impact on the events in the red-light district, but he really was just a fringe player. He took advantage of the lower criminal elements that mixed in the vice circles. They were his prey. They were gullible and looking for quick scores. Henkel knew how to manipulate this type of person and he did with ease even when he was suspected of murdering one or more in the circle of friends.

Henkel's Early Criminal Career

He was first arrested in 1960 at the age of 22 for robbing a service station. He received a sentence of 1-3 year. Henkel next shows up on the police blotter for stealing cigarettes in 1965.

His next brush with the law was a year later for stolen credit cards. He was caught impersonating a United States Steel executive. He had bought a car and had the paperwork delivered to his office. Police intercepted and tacked on a mail fraud charge.

His next caper looked to be the one that would put him on ice. Henkel and Andrew Russman robbed a bank on Mt. Washington in 1969. They got away with $80,000 and dumped the getaway car in the West End. They may have also stolen lesser sums from two other banks in the area as part of the spree.

Investigators traced some of the money from the bank robbery to a deposit at another bank in the North Hills. The account was opened by Henkel. They found him hiding with Russman in a West Mifflin motel under assumed names. Henkel was charged with the robbery. Russman only with harboring a fugitive.

By the time the trial came up, Russman was listed as missing. If investigators would have probed further, they may have uncovered that Henkel had murdered Russman. Henkel would reveal the location of his body in 1984.

Witnesses testified that Henkel was one of two men that were spotted leaving the getaway car in the West End. The other was likely Russman and the bank had Henkel's signature on the safety deposit box containing the marked money as well.

Henkel had tried to confuse witnesses during a police lineup. He was wearing a toupee during the robbery and refused to put it back on for the lineup. The defense also called a surprise witness in the hopes of exonerating Henkel. Peter Biagiarelli, a friend of Henkel, took the stand, already facing murder charges in a separate trial. He said that he and another unnamed fugitive stole the money and gave it to Henkel for safe keeping.

The jury did not believe the story and sentenced Henkel to 20 years in federal prison. He was sent to prison in Marion, Indiana. Authorities only recovered $20,000 of the approximately $123,000 stolen in the three robberies. Henkel provided no details on the missing money.

After the successful conviction, investigators did not follow up on Russman's disappearance, the other two robberies or the other case pending against Henkel – he had also stolen large amounts of stamps and was facing mail fraud charges again.

Henkel's time in Marion is both truth and legend. The truth part of the story is the prison documented Henkel as a model prisoner. His work in the health ward was a benefit for all and was just one example of how Henkel was a better person. In fact, Henkel was considered a model for the reform possible in prison.

Legend has it that Henkel was also able to further his own criminal education. He may have met another individual at this time who becomes part of the story but is never mentioned by name. This new associate had a working knowledge of explosives.

In the mid Seventies, the Federal government was giving out pardons to reduce inmate populations. In 1975, Richard Henkel was back in Pittsburgh, after serving only 4 years of his 20-year sentence.
That would be a mistake.

Sue Dixon

Then US Attorney Richard Thornburgh stated on Henkel's and other convicted robbers release, "Something is wrong when men sentenced to 20 years are out in a matter of months." It was a prescient statement.

When Henkel returned to Pittsburgh, he looked up a former childhood friend, Edgewood Police Officer Gary Small. Henkel's family had taken in Small after his father died when he was a boy. Small returned the favor, giving Henkel a place to stay. Small would be forever linked to Henkel, providing him guns, a proving ground and maybe support on some of his capers.

Small was the President of the Braddock Sportsmen Club in Washington Township, Westmoreland County. The club had ceased regular operations, but still owned a large, wooded area. Henkel used the old gun club to test out guns and bombs. It also became a burial ground where he stashed some of his corpses, including his old partner, Russman. He relocated the body to this area in 1975.

Wooded area in Westmoreland County that served as Henkel's "graveyard"

Henkel gravitated to the Court Lounge upon his return to Pittsburgh. If you were looking for a potential caper or wanted to meet other criminal elements, it was a good place to start. There he met Sue Dixon; she was managing the bar at the time.

Dixon was connected to the massage parlors. She was friends with the working girls, including Sasha Scott and Debbie Dremsek. She caught Henkel's eye, and they began dating. Shortly after this, Glenn Scott was murdered.

Dixon and Henkel set up house together in a Brentwood apartment. Scott soon moved in with them after her husband's death. Outwardly, Dixon and Henkel were a happy couple. Away from the public eye, that might not have been the case.

Dixon had to know what was going on as she watched people that she considered her friends die. After, Glenn and Sasha Scott and likely Bobby Pugh, she remained with Henkel. She named him the beneficiary of her estate and three separate insurance policies.

Henkel and Dixon got engaged and moved to an apartment in the West End after the Court Lounge closed. Henkel took a job managing Jeff's bar, a block away on South Main Street. Dixon had a job at Christopher's, a fine dining establishment on Mt. Washington.

On May 23, 1978, five months after Sasha Scott's death, Dixon was found in the trunk of a car in New Kensington. She was shot seven times with a .22 caliber weapon and stabbed 17 times with her throat slashed from side to side. She was also found to be 3 months pregnant.

Because of Dixon's connections to Scott and other vice figures, investigators believed her murder was related to the battle for control of the rackets. Starting with George Lee's murder and connected with those of Scott and massage parlor manager Bobby Pugh.

Henkel had thought this one through and he diverted suspicion away by reporting Sue Dixon as missing. He said Dixon had driven him to the airport a few days ago for business trip to the west coast. He claims to have spoken to her over the phone once but then could not reach her. He reported her missing when he supposedly returned from the trip.

Medical examiners estimated she had been dead 5 or 6 days before she was found. Henkel's story was plausible. Even though Dixon's family fought him, he was still paid the balance of Dixon's estate, including an uncashed paid check from Christopher's. He also collected on the insurance policies, while playing the part of grieving fiancé.

Dixon's murder case would remain open. She was 33.

Debbie Gentile

Debbie Gentile married young and divorced quick. She had a hard, short life. Bouncing around from Pittsburgh bar to bar, she held a variety of positions as barmaid, bartender, and manager. She was in and out of financial problems.

She may have been introduced to Henkel by Dixon or Scott. Her brother said she answered an ad for Jeff's bar where Henkel was the manager. Henkel hired her on before Dixon went missing.

In an affidavit filed in Henkel's subsequent murder trial, the county's homicide chief stated that Dixon and Gentile were reported to not be friendly and were more like enemies. Perhaps, Henkel was showing affection to Gentile, and maybe Dixon considered her a rival.

Two months after Dixon was found dead, Gentile sought psychological help at West Penn Hospital. Her relationship with Henkel became strained and they fought openly. After one altercation in January of 1979, Henkel fired Gentile.

Gentile was in financial distress and in severe depression. She and Henkel reconciled in March, and he gave her a great new job. He was sending her out to work with his partner in California, Jack Siggson, as a jewelry courier and salesperson. The job came with a new car.

About two months before Gentile took off for California, Henkel convinced her that she needed an insurance policy. Obtaining her signature, he took out the most outlandish policy of his many schemes. Gentile was now insured for $800,000 by the Airlines Passenger Association if she were to die on an airplane or on airplane property. The policy's beneficiary was Henkel's mom. Henkel paid $340.00 for the policy out of his own pocket.

Gentile's family was concerned about her all the time, but especially upon hearing she was leaving for California. Gentile told them that Henkel was into something big and knew lots of big people.

Jack Siggson was no boy scout. He had already served 6 years in a New Jersey prison for 2nd degree murder. It was a jewelry trading business that he and Henkel began, and it probably was moving stolen jewels along with legitimate transactions. Gentile was likely unaware and likely a perfect courier as she would likely allay suspicions.

Gentile was not in California very long before Henkel asked Siggson to put her on a plane back to Pittsburgh. Apparently, Henkel had decided that Gentil did know too much about his business dealings and that killing her would serve two purposes, removing her as a potential liability and collecting the large sum of money on her insurance policy.

Siggson would later testify that Henkel told him that insurance companies were one of the best ways to make money. He offered Siggson $50,000 and told him to give Gentile the plane fare to Pittsburgh.

Siggson told Gentile that Henkel wanted her back in Pittsburgh. Gentile was concerned, telling Siggson that Henkel was going to kill her. Yet, she let Siggson drive her to the airport with no luggage and without notifying any relatives that she would be back in Pittsburgh by morning.

Hours after her plane landed, her body was found in room 239 in the Greater Pittsburgh Airport Hotel located in the main terminal. She had 3 wounds to her head inflicted by a .22 caliber gun. She was stabbed 68 times in her neck and chest. Her throat was also slashed.

Henkel was the lead suspect. They tracked Gentile back to Siggson as well. Siggson originally refused to testify. The insurance company refused to pay, hoping the investigation would demonstrate that Henkel was the murderer and cited inconsistencies with the policy. They had their underwriter, Lloyd's of London, backing their claims of fraud.

Finally, on October 23, 1980, well over a year after Gentile's murder, officers from Allegheny County, Hampton Township and the Federal Bureau of Alcohol, Tobacco and Firearms converged on Henkel's house at 7:30 AM at 2305 West Hardies Road. They surprised him and took him into custody without a shot fired.

Henkel asked arresting officers to use the upstairs bathroom. Officers smartly denied his request. In a search of the house, they found a gun under the bed in an upstairs room. Henkel was charged with the murder of Debbie Gentile.

House where Henkel was arrested

He would soon find out that his associates who were still living were had been convinced to testify against him. He was unable to reach Siggson, who had disappeared into protective custody. Henkel, however, was not done yet.

Attempted Jail Break

Henkel was being held in Western State Penitentiary (West Pen) on the northside of Pittsburgh while he awaited trial. The District Attorney had already announced that he would seek the death penalty for Gentile's murder and was compiling evidence on additional murders.

The defense planned to call Louis Coviello, a convicted murderer serving time in West Pen, and John Dooley, a convicted robber already serving a 30–60-year prison term. The men were going to take credit for the murders of Gentile and Dixon.

Henkel and Coviello were being transferred from the prison to the courthouse for a hearing on the case. Henkel apparently did not want to wait to see what would happen in court. As they were brought into the final room for a search, prison guard Daniel Kohut noticed a bulge in Henkel's shoe.

Henkel produced two guns, one from each shoe that had somehow been smuggled to him. He attempted to take Kohut prisoner. He called for Coviello and both men subdued Kohut and a Kostas Mastos, a data processing supervisor, who happened to be in the search area before additional guards could respond.

Henkel did not make it out of the prison. Instead, he and Coviello took the two men hostage in a small room off the search area. They were able to barricade the door and forced the prison to call in its negotiating team. Negotiators responded by turning off electricity and cold water to the area. Hot water was still available as the line supplied the entire facility and as such could not be turned off. Negotiations went on for 5 1/2 days.

Negotiators also withheld food. Rather than conceding, Henkel upped the stakes. Henkel fashioned a noose from what was available in the room and threatened to hang Kohut. Food was brought in and Kohut gave Coviello, who liked to eat, his piece of cake in a gesture of goodwill.

Tensions were high and both the captors and captives suffered from a severe lack of sleep. At one point, Mastos shouted for cigarettes, and they were delivered through a slot in the door. Kohut reported that on several occasions, Henkel strung him up and he had to stand on his tiptoes for hours at a time to survive the noose.

On the morning of the 6th day, negotiators had secured the release of Matos. Coviello came out with him, apparently, he had enough. Henkel became more panicked. He expected guards to storm the room at any minute to end the siege. Henkel told Kohut that he was going to kill him and then himself.

The prison negotiators and staff remained calm and have been lauded for the efforts on how they handled the situation. They were able to bring it to a successful end by having Coviello call Henkel and tell him that he was not harmed and was handled gently after his surrender.

Henkel opened the door, releasing Kohut who was shaken but otherwise not harmed. He was taken back into custody. Authorities wasted no time, they transferred him to Lewisburg Federal Penitentiary, a high security prison in the easter part of Pennsylvania. Prison guard, Roy Layne would later be convicted of supplying the guns to Henkel.

Over Henkel's objections, the judge also moved his trial to Philadelphia. The hostage situation was front page news for several weeks and there was very little hope in finding an impartial jury for the trial.

Just before the trial, Henkel was again transferred, this time to the state prison outside of Philadelphia. The DA had stated several times that he had enough evidence to convict Henkel on Gentile's murder and the potential to prove additional crimes, including murder. However, the day before the trial was to begin, the DA was at the prison accepting Henkel's signature on a plea bargain.

Henkel would serve life in prison without the opportunity for parole.

Investigation and Other Odd Bits

As part of the plea bargain, Henkel secured charges would be dropped against his brother Robert. Robert was facing charges of aiding and abetting. He had been caught trying to smuggle guns to Henkel for what may have been another planned escape before the West Pen incident.

In addition, Henkel was to provide information on four additional murders. As Debbie Gentile and Sue Dixon were essentially already proven, the additional information was assumed to include the murders of Andrew Russman, Bruce Agnew, Glenn Scott, and Sasha Scott.

During Siggson's testimony, several interesting charges were also leveled against Henkel. The most outlandish, was a plot to strap a bomb to Pittsburgh Steelers' patriarch Arthur Rooney. The plan was to hold him for ransom with the ability to detonate the bomb remotely.

Worrying that Rooney's advanced age might cause a heart attack and thus foil the ransom collection, the caper was shifted to Edward Ryan, founder of Ryan Homes. Siggson testified that he cased Ryan's home more than ten times, though it was not carried through.

Small and Agnew were also linked to the bomb plot. Small would defend himself against the accusations and other charges for years. Agnew wasn't so lucky. He was murdered at the same location where the explosives were tested, the old gun club.

Siggson also portrayed Henkel as being paranoid. He said Henkel wore a bullet proof vest around the house and once shot at his reflection in a mirror because he thought someone was there.

After Henkel left his Philadelphia prison on the way back to federal prison at Marion, his cell was searched. Henkel may have been planning yet another escape. Three keys to handcuffs and 4 ft section of wire were found. Guards were unhappy with the plea bargain, imagining what the wire could have done to one of them.

Henkel, a Contract Killer?

After his arrest for the Gentile murder, Henkel is often referred to in news stories as a contract killer. There is circumstantial evidence to support this claim, but no hard evidence that he worked as a hired hitman or killed for anyone but his own desires and benefit.

Legend has it that John LaRocca, head of the Pittsburgh family at the time, supposedly asked Henkel how much money it would take for Henkel to leave him alone. There is no evidence linking him to the Pittsburgh crime family other than he hung out at the Court Lounge, which was run by its members.

There appears to be a few connections to the Cleveland crime family, however. This would have been cause for concern in Pittsburgh as they were in the middle of a turf war, primarily for control of Youngstown, Ohio. Henkel's mom had moved there while he was in prison.

Known Youngstown hitman, Joe DeRose, lived with Henkel. Small did business with him and other Ohio mobsters, supplying guns. DeRose went missing in 1981. When Henkel was arrested, notes that were passed between his brothers and him mentioned prominent Ohio crime figures as well.

Henkel may have admitted to 27 or possibly 32 murders. However, these were the murders that investigators questioned him about:

George Lee- Lee's murder was still on authority minds at the time. It was a contract murder, likely organized by the Pittsburgh crime family with Nick DeLucia possibly playing a role. It was carried out by two shooters is does not necessarily match the Henkel pattern. It could have been possible that Henkel was one of the shooters. Perhaps, Small or someone else was a partner. However, it is more likely that DeLucia selected shooters close to him, including his brother-in-law. Henkel never admitted to participating.

Glenn Scott – Glenn was Sasha's husband and dubious businessman. He was gunned down in 1975 at a stable in the northern suburbs. He was found with 15 shotgun wounds, 10 of them to the head. Henkel supposedly confessed to this murder, and it fits his pattern of multiple gunshots particularly to the head. Henkel did not use a shotgun in other murders, but it may have been handy or provided for him. Two men were reportedly seen leaving the stables so Henkel may not have been alone. Scott's family has never been given a definitive report by authorities stating Henkel was the murderer, even though Henkel was connected to an insurance policy and gave information after pleading guilty to the Gentile murder.

Sasha Scott – Sasha's story was told earlier. Henkel was suspected in providing the bomb that was delivered to the Gemini and killed her. Scott was a friend of Dixon's and lived with her and Henkel for a time. Henkel was paid on an insurance policy in her name after her death. Glenn Scott's relatives were never formally told that Henkel was the murderer of Sasha either, despite Henkel reportedly giving evidence to authorities as part of his plea bargain.

Anthony "Bobby" Pugh – Pugh was murdered in his apartment. He was the manager of a massage parlor in Brentwood. Henkel was living with Dixon and Scott in Brentwood at the time. Pugh's murder was originally investigated as being connected to George Lee's death and the subsequent battle for control of the vice rackets between DeLucia and Dante "Tex" Gill. However, he was found with six bullet wounds to the head by a .22 caliber gun. Henkel used a .22 in the murders of Dixon and Gentile, and the multiple gun shots to the head fits his pattern as well.

Pugh was friends with Scott, Dixon, and Debbie Dremsek. Pugh's wife was out with Dremsek when he was murdered. Henkel may have had an insurance policy on Pugh as well. Though never announced, Pugh's murder was likely committed by Henkel.

Andrew Russman – Henkel's probable first murder. He led authorities to an old gun club in Westmoreland County where he claims to have moved Russman's body when he was released from prison in 1975. Russman's body was not found as development had begun in the area and his body may have been inadvertently removed during excavations.

Bruce Agnew – Agnew was one of the partners on a bomb scheme to take Art Rooney hostage. He was taken to the gun club and unknowingly dug his own grave. He was shot on site and buried. Henkel led authorities to Agnew's grave and his body was recovered.

Joseph DeMarco – DeMarco was a bookmaker and was owner of the Court Lounge before George Lee and Anthony Lagatutta. He was found in 1980 in a car parked at the Greater Pittsburgh Airport parking lot. His body was riddled with bullets. This murder intrigues me as the body was found at the airport with multiple gunshot wounds – fitting Henkel's patterns. However, it was reported that Henkel did not confess. This murder would have earned Henkel the contract killer title used after his name if confirmed.

There just is not enough evidence to prove that Henkel also worked as a contract killer for someone other than himself. Coupling that with Henkel's unpredictability and particularly public escapades would likely discount his use. There was just too much risk.

Henkel at times looks like a master criminal. At other times, he looks clumsy and was often easily caught. He may have been caught sooner into his killing spree if not hidden in the veil of the vice rackets that captured investigator's attention while they totally missed the serial killer that was hiding in plain sight in a bar on the West End's Main Street.

It was almost if Henkel wanted to be caught. Perhaps, he just thought himself invincible and able to slip away whenever he chose.

Henkel's Return to Pittsburgh

Henkel was brough back to Pittsburgh in the summer of 1984. Over the objections of Small, the gun club had been sold to two men who planned a housing development in the rural area off State Route 66.

Henkel had agreed to lead authorities to at least two graves on the site. Henkel was heavily shackled and guarded. His memory was not great and the area to be searched was large. Still on July 19th, Bruce Agnew was found.

The morning of July 20th, the cavalcade of cars was set to make the drive with Henkel to continue the search for Russman. They got an anonymous call that urged caution with the second grave, as it may be boobytrapped with an explosive device and that Henkel's former associates may either be planning a breakout or revenge with an attack on the search party.

Henkel confirmed that the body may have indeed been wired with an explosive, but not by him. The unnamed associate re-entered the Henkel story here. Authorities took no chances, deploying bomb sniffing dogs and metal detector. Henkel took no chances as well – he refused to ride in the first car.

The search did not turn up any explosives or Russman's body. It was likely disturbed by an excavator working on the site towards the road and removed to another site where it is now gone forever. Luckily, there was no explosion.

Henkel disappears from the public eye into his life in prison. At some point, he was moved to SCI Greene County, Pennsylvania's maximum-security prison. Ironically, the prison also houses the state's death row. Henkel is that close to what was once thought to be his fate.

20 Another Tragic Last Supper

Mike Kalina is dead. That is the tragedy. All the rest – the speculation about motive, the apparent ethical lapses, the intriguing cast of characters, the fragmentary reports from law enforcement offices and the gossip is subordinate. – John Craig, Publisher, The Pittsburgh Post-Gazette

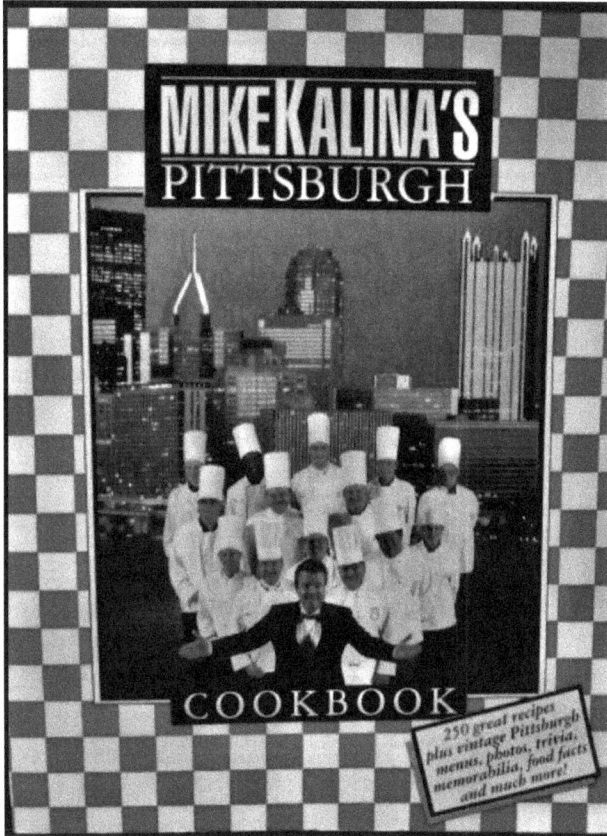

Mike Kalina's death is a tragedy and even more than 20 years later, the speculation into why it happened continues. We may never understand the cause, but to even begin to understand, we must examine all the subordinate information that Mr. Craig asked his readers to look past.

Kalina joined the Post-Gazette in 1971. He worked his way up and was named the paper's food critic in 1978. It was in this job that he excelled and has left a lasting mark on the Pittsburgh food scene. He was affable, funny, charming, and very charismatic. His personality came through in his columns and his notoriety grew.

Readers trusted him. Restauranters coveted his reviews, hoping for five forks, a rating system that he invented. He, in-turn, was dedicated to improving Pittsburgh's food scene. He hoped to elevate it above the infamous greasy spoons to fine dining.

His good looks and good humor translated to television as well. Even with his talents for the written word, he excelled on the screen, beginning with a phantom diner segment in 1989 on KDKA-TV.

His fame grew outside of Pittsburgh as well. He wrote two weekly columns, *The Lazy Gourmet* and *The Travelin Gourmet,* which appeared in 25 newspapers across the country. At the time of his death, he was in negotiations to syndicate two different television shows nationally.

Kalina did not stop there. He helped found a culinary institute in Pittsburgh and published a cookbook of Pittsburgh recipes. He was also working on a screenplay. If this gives the impression that Kalina was riding high, well that would be a correct assumption.

Kalina worked at a frenetic pace, some would say neurotic. In his eulogy, Kalina was described as a gourmet and gourmand, travel writer, music critic, playwright, photographer, songwriter, scriptwriter, lyricist, pianist, columnist, television personality, comedian, and even blind-folded chess master. That is a lot of talent.

He had tremendous concern for his reputation. He also was someone that did not let obstacles stand in his way. That drive and some friends with dubious reputations and one with his own motives would, in the end, be Kalina's undoing.

Many restauranters became friends with Kalina, even those that did not get a spectacular review. Joseph Costanzo, Jr., the owner of Primadonna's restaurant in Stowe, hounded him for more than 2 years for a review. Kalina was pleasantly surprised when he finally drove out to the restaurant and the two became friends.

Because of these friendships and other business dealings, Kalina always walked a fine ethical line with his job as a reviewer. However, several restaurant owners reported that he always turned down free meals and drinks, saying the paper paid for his dining.

The first questionable ethical lapse happened in 1989 for his wedding. Several restaurants sent dishes for the reception at the Sheraton. When questioned about the activity, the restaurants said that Kalina's wife, Doris, had asked them as a surprise for Kalina. Sarris Candies provided a tray of chocolates, telling investigators Kalina never reviewed them or had any reason to as they were not a restaurant. "This was a wedding gift."

Where things really got out of control was the cookbook. It was a labor of love for Kalina, celebrating Pittsburgh's culture and history. The cookbook features 250 recipes, 80 photos, Pittsburgh trivia, and even vintage menus from local restaurants. It was available at the now defunct Kaufmann's Department store for $18.95 and via mail order.

It was not cheap to print and Kalina did not seem to have the funds to see it through. The paper provided no monetary support, though the Post-Gazette did advertise it and was very proud that their food critic had produced it. They also helped launch it with a gala that benefitted charity. Kalina faced setbacks trying to get the book published. He approached Anthony Lagattuta for advice. You might remember him from the first story in the book. Lagattuta was also a partner in Keystone Mailing Service, a direct marketing firm. Kalina tried to raise revenue by marketing recipes and selling kitchen utensils through the mail. Lagattuta reported this was not very successful.

However, Lagattuta liked Kalina and called him his friend, introducing him to another friend, Rocco Ferrone. Ferrone was the production manager at K-Con printing in Sharpsburg. Kalina now had a printer. Rocco happened to be the brother of Augie Ferrone, a well-known bookmaker.

At some point Kalina also partnered with Lou Adams. Adams owned a restaurant consulting firm and agreed to help Kalina fundraise for the cookbook and market it. Adams began developing marketing packages for restaurants to be included – for a price.

Most restaurants jumped at the chance to be included. Not only was it an opportunity to help out Kalina, a friend and someone they respected for helping grow Pittsburgh's culinary scene, but they also saw the marketing benefits. Some believed they were also helping charity as Adams did say profits were being donated.

Kalina and Adams approached at least one local charity to see if they would provide some of the upfront costs. The local office for Make A Wish passed on the opportunity, explaining they could not provide funding for the project even if the profits would come back to the organization.

The cookbook project was certainly difficult, but true to his nature, Kalina did manage to get it printed and released. The glitzy launch gala was a party to be at, and restauranters and the public ponied up for the $100 tickets.

The Post-Gazette was not aware that Kalina and Adams had put together the marketing packages for inclusion in the cookbook. If they were, this might have been a red flag as a possible ethics infraction. It may have meant that Kalina would have lost his position at the paper or would have to be reassigned. Still, he was only working part time anyways.

The Smithfield Café would end up being the smoking gun. Kalina had reviewed the establishment and though the review was not negative, he did criticize the service. The Café is no longer there, but those I related the story to, commented that the service was indeed subpar typically.

However, the owner of the Café, John Petrolias, was not happy and made a phone call to a friend of his, U.S District Attorney Tom Corbett. Corbett was fresh off a huge victory. He had just put eight members of the Pittsburgh family of La Cosa Nostra in jail in the first Racketeer Influenced and Corrupt Organizations Act (RICO) trial in Pittsburgh.

He had seriously crippled the organization by nabbing two underbosses, Charles Porter and Luis Raucci. He had not killed it though, as he did not manage to incriminate the head of the family at the time, Michael Genovese.

Petrolias told Corbett that he had heard rumors that Kalina and Adams were selling favorable reviews. Corbett had hoped to use Kalina to expose information on possible hidden interests by those in the family in at least 4 area restaurants.

One of those restaurants was D'Imperio's, owned by Anthony D'Imperio. Kalina had given the restaurant his highest 5 fork rating and he and D'Imperio had become friends. The restaurant was a longtime client of Adams' and paid approximately $1,000 to be included in the cookbook as well.

D'Imperio's was also mentioned during the RICO trial. Philip Leonetti testified that restaurant served as a meeting place for the Pittsburgh and Philadelphia crime families in 1986. Leonetti, a high-ranking member of the Philadelphia family had turned state's evidence and was key witness during the Pittsburgh trial.

This was enough of a connection for Corbett to set up a sting. He had Petrolias set up a meeting at his other restaurant, Jamie's on the Square in Market Square. Corbett's team of investigators listened in as Adams promised a 4-fork rating for Jamie's for $2,000, saying part of the money would go to Kalina.

The feds used this information to expand the investigation. They subpoenaed a half dozen restaurants, questioning about the marketing fees for the cookbook as well as any other benefits. They also investigated Rocco Ferrone and Anthony Lagattuta.

Though Ferrone had an infamous uncle, it was clear he was not involved in anything illegal. Lagattuta was also cleared. He commented, "Whatever reputation I had, has certainly lost its luster. Do I still qualify as an organized crime figure?"

Kalina had heard about the subpoenas. Just days after they had been delivered, he was sitting in Primadonna's with Costanzo. Costanzo later detailed that Kalina was visibly nervous and told him the advertising fees were legal but that they were not ethical. He was worried about losing his job. "He said he was going to go to the grand jury and tell them the truth and not ask for anything," said Costanzo. That was Thursday, January 24, 1992.

There is much speculation as to what happened in the intervening days until 8:00 am on Monday, January 27th when police found his body. One story has Kalina meeting with Adams in a bar on the South Side. Adams purportedly suggested that Kalina should get a good lawyer.

Sometime on Sunday, Kalina purchased a green garden hose, a utility knife, and a roll of duct tape from a hardware store. He then drove to the former Baltimore and Ohio railroad at 704 Second Avenue.

Police found the hose running from the tailpipe of his car to the rear window. The opening had been sealed inside and out with duct tape. Kalina was slumped over in the driver's seat. The car was no longer running, but the ignition key was turned to the on position. Police believe it ran out of gas sometime during the night.

There were two empty beer cans in the car. Kalina's leather jacket was draped over the passenger seat, covering a partially used roll of tape and a utility knife. The coroner pronounced him dead in parking lot, later releasing the cause of death as carbon monoxide poisoning. Kalina was just 49 years old and left behind a wife and two daughters, one just 16 months old.

Kalina's death, especially with an open federal investigation, sparked several theories for his suicide, and he was tried in public long before any testimony even began. His funeral was attended by restauranters, tv personalities and even Mayor Sophie Masloff.

Adams would later testify to the grand jury, under immunity, that Kalina and he split less than $10,000 over 5 years from selling reviews to approximately half a dozen restaurants. Kalina's friends and family believe that Adams was lying and that Kalina did not know everything that Adams was up to, using Kalina's name. And they have a case.

No restaurant owner ever came forward to implicate Kalina. Still, the investigation drug on for more than two years. Corbett steadfastly refused to confirm or deny the existence of a probe as was his office's privilege. He would only say that Kalina would obviously not be indicted, without ever officially clearing him of wrongdoing.

John Craig, Kalina's editor at the paper, doggedly pursued Corbett without much success. He conducted his own investigation and found that though Kalina made some obvious ethical infractions, but there was absolutely no evidence to support criminal charges. Craig went us far to blame Corbett for his actions that may have contributed to the suicide, going so far as to speculate that Kalina would still be alive had Corbett just contacted the paper with the allegations rather than pursuing an indictment that wasted a lot of taxpayer money in the process, when there were far bigger white-collar crimes going on in the city.

"We are not responsible for other's actions, only ourselves," responded Corbett. "We have acted responsibly." Corbett went on to serve as Governor of Pennsylvania. He is perhaps best known for criticism of how he handled the investigation of convicted sex abuser Jerry Sandusky.

The case against Kalina still does not make sense. Why would he risk everything for a piece of $10,000, especially when his pending syndication deals held the promise of hundreds of thousands if not millions of potential income. Why worry about losing a part time job when more was waiting?

His wife, Doris, came forward with another piece of evidence. She said Kalina had just learned that he had been diagnosed with throat cancer. This was a second occurrence, Kalina recovered from a similar cancer early in his life. Doris said the latest diagnosis hit him hard and that he was depressed. For a man so driven to succeed with so much talent, a federal investigation, a significant health issue, an uncertain future, and maybe most of all, a tarnished reputation may have just been too much to take at that time. Perhaps Kalina's friend and fellow author, Barry Paris, summed it up best in his eulogy. "The fact that a set of vicious and unproven allegations might have put him over the edge, does not mean that they are true."

21 The Gentleman of Verona

Michael Genovese used to tell his girlfriend that they had the wrong guy every time his name would show up in the local papers. "That is some other Michael Genovese." That was plausible as he was often mistaken as the Michael Genovese that was head of the New York crime family of the same name. Papers often mistakenly mentioned that Pittsburgh's Michael Genovese was related to New York's as well.

All this misdirection served Genovese well as he kept law enforcement stumbling to connect him to crimes and kept him out of prison. Genovese was perhaps the last great boss of the Pittsburgh crime family, expanding its reach and income as the heads of crime families in New York and Philadelphia were being sent away for long prison sentences.

Genovese was born in 1919 and grew up in the East Liberty neighborhood, a once hot bed for organized crime. He started in the numbers racket and worked his way up during the golden age of organized crime under Sebastian John LaRocca's growing Pittsburgh crime family.

In his early years, he was arrested for robbery and carrying concealed weapons. He also served time for contempt for not testifying, even though he was granted immunity. Genovese was low-key and often reclusive, especially as he rose in the ranks.

John LaRocca, head of the family, trusted Genovese to carry out family business. In 1967, Genovese likely organized the hit on Alphonse Marano. Marano had mistakenly brought an Internal Revenue Service agent into Joseph Pecora's West Virginia operations. Pecora was an underboss and was responsible for his own territory for the family.

The contract supposedly went to Nick "The Blade" Gesuale. Gesuale is infamous as the "Pittsburgh Connection" for Henry Hill and was featured in the *Goodfellas* film. He bragged that this hit was how he made his "bones" in the mob, earning induction into the family. Whether or not that story is true, Gesuale was the largest narcotics trafficker in Pittsburgh and funneled a lot of cash into the family and up to Genovese.

In 1971, police investigated the murder of Genovese's younger brother, Fiore, outside of a social club known to be a hangout for organized crime. Fiore was gunned down on the street and police thought it could have been a gangland hit possibly over illegal gambling debts. However, investigators found it very sloppy, and it turned out that the perpetrator was someone that hung around the club and was often bullied.

Genovese rose to be one of LaRocca's top lieutenants which included Joseph Pecora and Kelly Mannarino. Genovese kept his base in East Liberty and may have even been considered the "Street Boss" at times. Pecora ran operations West Virginia and Mannarino's base was in New Kensington.

The three became a ruling triumvirate when LaRocca went into semi-retirement in 1978. LaRocca left the Pittsburgh cold for sunny Florida after decades leading the family, seeing it flourish and prosper.

In other areas of the country and especially across the state in Philadelphia, there were power struggles going on for top leaders. Many of these were settled with violence and with more and more bodies being found riddled with bullets or blown up in the case of Philadelphia, increasingly drawing the attention of law enforcement.

In Pittsburgh the three kept their heads, respecting each other's territories, agreeing that money was the most important thing. Still as LaRocca was getting up in age, there was a question of who would be the next leader.

That was settled naturally. Mannarino died of cancer in 1980. Around the same time Pecora went away to prison for several years. Genovese became the defacto boss in waiting, carrying out LaRocca's orders.

Genovese was growing restless, unable to put his expansion ideas into practice. He still had potential rivals in the family and was facing his own health issues. In 1982, citing serious health issues, the Pennsylvania Organized Crime Commission did not believe Genovese would rise to boss and that there was a lull in activity in Pittsburgh. Pecora was due to be released from prison and the commission believed he or a younger member might overtake Genovese for the job.

The Commission got it wrong. Genovese seemed to use the lull to fly under the radar of law enforcement and to consolidate his power in the organization. LaRocca died in 1985 and the 1988 Commission report acknowledged Genovese as the head of the family.

Genovese breathed new life in the family. He expanded the family's narcotics interests, and drugs destined for other areas of the country often were routed through Pittsburgh for distribution. He also added video poker on top of the traditional illegal gambling operations. Both proved to be very lucrative.

In 1990, Genovese began taking over the operations of the Cleveland crime family. Cleveland was a long-time rival and turf battles had been ongoing between the families, particularly in Youngstown, Ohio, where both families operated. Genovese successfully consolidated power, expanding the Pittsburgh family's footprint.

Genovese kept himself insulated from operations. Money was hand delivered to him by the same person. He also moved his headquarters out of Pittsburgh, heading up the Allegheny River to the quieter hamlet of Verona. He set up shop in a small used car lot, LA Motors. This gave him a job cover as well. He also shrewdly invested illegal proceeds into real estate across the region.

The success, particularly drug trafficking, would eventually wake law enforcement. Genovese did not have to worry much about local law, as he had considerable influence. His driveway at his home in Deer Lakes was paved at the county's expense.

The Feds were a different story. The FBI and federal prosecutors were coming off a huge win in the Mafia Commission trial in New York, which secured incarceration of family bosses for the first time. The government had finally figured out how to use the Racketeer Influenced and Corrupt Organizations Act or RICO. And they were sharing it with other areas of the country in the hopes that more cases would be brought.

Pieces were starting to fall in place. Joey Rosa, a drug trafficker for the family, was arrested in 1988. Facing a long prison sentence for running a large cocaine ring, he began to talk. The feds set up electronic surveillance of LA Motors in 1988, expanding their wiretaps in 1990. Genovese was meeting daily at that location with his two top lieutenants, Charles Porter, and Luis Raucci.

Rosa was third generation in the Pittsburgh family. He was a good money earner, but either through his underlings or his own missteps found himself in hot water. Rosa was summoned to a meeting at the former Holiday House in Monroeville, a favorite meeting space of the family. Rosa had come into possession of few items that were taken from Mannarino's house during his funeral (more on that in the next chapter).

Rosa said he was given these items to pay off a drug debt and did have knowledge that they were stolen – well at least not from Mannarino. Genovese believed his story and pardoned him. This may have been a mistake on his part.

The Feds wiretaps caught a lot of information. On one tape, Raucci asked Genovese for accounting advice on how to hide his income as he knew the IRS was investigating him. In all, 12 transcripts would become part of the government's first RICO trial in Pittsburgh.

None of those transcripts incriminated Genovese, however. Both Porter and Raucci as well as seven other defendants stood trial on murder and drug charges with Rosa and Philip Leonetti of the Philadelphia family.

Former LA Motors car dealership in Verona, PA
The Feds placed wiretaps to try and catch Genovese

Genovese was smart enough to not say anything about his involvement within the car dealership, taking walks around the neighborhood with Porter and Raucci. Investigators attempted to plant listening devices in the trees and traffic poles along the route with no luck. Raucci did call him boss on one of the tapes, but it was not enough to build a case.

Rosa apparently did not give up Genovese either. In a conversation that Genovese supposedly had with Rosa's grandfather, Joseph Sica, he reassured him that it was not his fault his grandson had talked. "We didn't go for that kind of thing," he purportedly said.

Genovese was not out of the woods. Charles Porter was the next to turn state's evidence. Porter's testimony was instrumental in trials against organized crime figures and drug trafficker across the country, demonstrating just how influential Pittsburgh was in the narcotics trade. Porter even saved the man that helped put him in prison, exposing a contract on Rosa's life.

Porter was interviewed and testified multiple times, securing an early release from prison. Through all of this, he never provided any evidence against Genovese. Tom Corbett, the US District Attorney for Pittsburgh and slew of investigators relentlessly tried to connect Genovese to a crime, any crime. Still, Genovese remained free.

Federal investigations were not the only thing working against the Pittsburgh family. Genovese was overseeing operations while fighting age and attrition throughout his ranks. He was not alone. After all the troubles organized crime had faced with more and higher-ranking figures breaking the code of *Omerta*, the ruling commission in New York decided to close ranks, preventing smaller families under their control from adding new members. Pittsburgh was able to replace a member that died or retired but was forbidden to grow.

Smaller families began folding into to larger families in New York or Chicago. If LaRocca oversaw the golden age, Genovese was the boss for the uncertain age. He deftly expanded operations with fewer resources, and he outwitted law enforcement where others were not so lucky.

Genovese passed away at age 87 after long illnesses of bladder cancer and heart disease. He was one of the last connections to the golden age of the mafia. He dressed meticulously, and his nails were manicured. He flew under the radar. He showed respect and was offered it.

He was shrewd and kept to the old code.

22 **Rob the Boss**

This is a tale of two eras of the Pittsburgh crime family.

Gabriel "Kelly" Mannarino represents the golden age. As a youngster, he was already making a name for himself as the nascent family was getting its start at the end of the Prohibition era. He rose through the ranks and often was referred to as the head of the Westmoreland County family, demonstrating the great trust, autonomy, and success that he had.

Representing the modern era is Joseph "Joey" Rosa. He was the third generation in the family following his father, Frank Rosa, and his grandfather, Joseph Sica. Rosa engineered the largest cocaine ring in Pittsburgh in the 1980's and his testimony in the first RICO trial in Pittsburgh decimated its ranks.

Mannarino may have known Joey as Frank's son. Rosa certainly knew Mannarino, maybe as LaRocca's boss in waiting. Their paths only crossed briefly. As Mannarino lay in a funeral home, Rosa robbed his house.

Mannarino started in the Northside gang that would eventually consolidate the smaller gangs in the region, culminating in the murder of John Volpe, into what became known as the Pittsburgh family. Mannarino cut his teeth in the numbers racket, and he was partners in a slot machine business with John LaRocca and Frank Amato in coin operated vending machine business as early as 1933.

Amato was one of the first bosses of the new family. He ceded control to LaRocca when his health declined. LaRocca ruled the family for more than 30 years and Mannarino was often cited as his number two. Mannarino even married one of Amato's daughters.

Mannarino established a power base in New Kensington in Westmoreland County together with his brother, Sam. Together they built up the largest gambling operation in the area, estimated to be worth $2 million. Sam died in 1967 and Kelly Mannarino took full control of the organization.

LaRocca brought Mannarino and Michael Genovese to the infamous Apalachin meeting in upstate New York in 1957. The historic mafia summit was organized by Vito Genovese (no relation to Michael) and attended by as many as 100 syndicate members from around the country. It caught the attention of local and state law enforcement when they noticed many expensive cars with out of state license plates invading the tiny hamlet of Apalachin.

All three Pittsburghers were arrested by authorities during the raid. Mannarino and LaRocca were issued subpoenas to testify before the grand jury tasked with investigating. Servers came to New Kensington, but Mannarino was nowhere to be found.

He supposedly boarded a boat to Italy, but his name was not on the passenger list. Some surmised that he was in Cuba. He was an investor in the Sans Suci Casino with Santo Trafficante Jr., head of the Tampa crime family, and Fugencio Bautista, the President of Cuba. Others speculated that he and LaRocca took a long vacation in Mexico, where they also had business interests.

The grand jury dropped the investigation with insufficient evidence to bring charges and Mannarino suddenly was back in New Kensington. When asked where he was, he replied, "Shangri-La".

Mannarino's casino featured craps and barboute tables on the second floor of Triangle Billiards on Barnes Street in New Kensington. There were also phones that could connect you to a bookmaker if you wanted to lay a bet. The casino was next to the Kenmar hotel. Valets parked your car in the adjacent city parking lot. Visitors came from around the country to test their luck in what was known as "Little Vegas".

To access the casino, you had to ascend stairs in the middle of the billiards hall. You had to be buzzed in through the heavy crash door, which also featured a mirror to allow the doorman to scrutinize you before allowing entry. Daniel "Speedo" Hanna was usually at the door.

John Fontana ran the casino operation. He also held a position on New Kensington's election board and served a suspended sentence for voter fraud. Mannarino was well connected politically and very well insulated from the day-to-day operations of the gambling den.

Federal law enforcement observed Mannarino in the casino from time to time, hosting big wigs or in the dice office reviewing operations. They eventually raided the casino but did not catch Mannarino. They did snag Pittsburgh Police Lieutenant Arthur Baker who happened to be in the casino at the time of the raid. The casino was back up and running soon after the raid.

Batista seems to have double crossed Mannarino, muscling him out of the casino in Cuba. Mannarino may have wanted revenge or perhaps running guns was just good business. Some heavy-duty arms, including large machine guns and assault rifles, disappeared from an Ohio National Guard armory and federal officials observed them being loaded on a small plane at a small airport near New Kensington.

The delivery truck had markings from a company owned by brother Sam. Officials waited for it to take off, later apprehending the pilot in Morgantown, West Virginia where it stopped for fuel. Amongst the delivery boys arrested in Pennsylvania was Sam's son-in-law and Speedo Hanna.

Authorities suspected the Mannarinos, but other than the close connections to those arrested, they had no other evidence. Oh, and Kelly had taken some time away from New Kensington anyway during the caper. The guns were destined for Fidel Castro's rebels. Castro did remove Batista from power and closed all the casinos. The situation created strange bedfellows between the CIA and the American mob, but that is a different story.

After Prohibition, labor unions were seen as a strong revenue source for crime families across the country. The mafia began to infiltrate the unions sometimes in partnership and sometimes, especially in Chicago, by force.

In Pittsburgh, it appears to be mostly in partnership with union leaders. The unions held significant cash in the form of welfare and pension funds collected from its membership. Using these funds, crime families could make high interest loans to individuals and companies at a huge profit.

The Teamsters union houses were most active in the schemes. The cooperation started at the top and filtered down to local leadership as well. In Pittsburgh, Nick Stirone, the local boss of Common Laborers got into hot water with the federal government. LaRocca and Mannarino were identified as possible associates.

LaRocca and Mannarino were summoned to testify in Washington, DC by none other than Robert Kennedy, the US Attorney General under his brother, President John F. Kennedy. Kennedy. A special committee grilled both on local ties as well as national scams involving the rackets and organized labor. Both cited the 5th Amendment often during testimony not wishing to incriminate themselves.

The feds could never convict Mannarino throughout his life. They said it was like trying to prove the existence of Santa Claus. Mannarino could not run from cancer though. It took him on July 11, 1980, at the age of 64.

Mannarino was laid out at John D. Giunta Funeral home in the New Kensington neighborhood of Arnold. His funeral was attended by family, local dignitaries, and out of towners alike. While people were paying the last respects across town, Mannarino's stately home at 540 Charles Avenue was being robbed. Who would have the gumption or sheer ignorance to rob a boss?

Joey Rosa was born into the mob. His grandfather, Joseph Sica was a legend in the family and highly respected. He was the only family member during the golden era to serve time on a federal charge. He did his time quietly and was a trusted advisor to LaRocca and Genovese after him.

Frank Rosa, Joey's father, was Sica's son-in-law. It would seem that Joey was destined for induction just based on his lineage. However, it also appears that his father and grandfather respected the old ways and were determined for Joey to earn his way in.

Joey earned a reputation as a loose cannon early on and never lost the title even as he progressed in the family. In his teens, Joey began using drugs at 12 and was selling by the age of 16. He would rob other dealers to get the money to buy more drugs.

Frank did not approve of his son's habits and Joey describes being beat with a baseball bat for his transgressions. Whether it was pressure, rebellion or privilege, Joey never seemed to respect the rules and traditions of the family even though he desired a position within it.

As Mannarino lay in the funeral home, it was likely Rosa and maybe some co-conspirators that robbed his house. They made off with some valuables, including jewelry, vases, and statues. Rosa would later be summoned to the Holiday House in Monroeville for questioning before Genovese and other leaders to answer for the robbery. Rosa admitted being in possession of the stolen goods bit a fellow dealer vouched that he had come into possession of them through another dealer that was paying off some debts. Genovese liked Rosa and let him off. The valuables were returned to Mannarino's widow.

It might have been different, or perhaps it was a blessing, that Frank Rosa died in 1982 – Joey was only 23. At least, Frank was not around to see what his son would notoriously accomplish. Joey went to live with his grandfather and began to be groomed by Luis Raucci, raised to one of Genovese's underbosses and former protégé of Sica.

Rosa caught the attention of Genovese and may have been officially inducted into the family after he staged a robbery of his own jewelry store in the Clark Building downtown. He scored $300,000 and kicked $30,000 to Genovese as a tribute.

Rosa and his partners began bringing in cocaine in 1984 from Miami, supplying it to dealers across the region. Raucci was making $10,000 for every kilo. When Rosa complained that was too steep, he was allowed to work under Charles Porter, Genovese's other underboss, for $2,000 per kilo.

Despite the tributes due, Rosa and his partners were raking in the dough and continued to grow the cocaine ring. Rosa was also shaking down other dealers, stealing money and drugs then capitalizing on his mob connections to discourage retribution.

In true "no honor amongst thieves" fashion, Rosa even cheated the family's major supplier, Ramon Sosa, out of $250,000. Porter was angry, asking incredulously, "you ripped off the Cuban?" Rosa got out of it by giving Porter most of the swindled funds.

In 1984, another clumsy swindler was introduced Rosa, Joseph Bertone. Bertone owned Joey's Restaurant in McKeesport, PA. He owed a lot of money to a people that you do not want to owe money to.

Joey's was firebombed in 1978. It was retribution from some people that did not like Bertone. It burned down again in 1982. That fire is unclear, and Bertone may have done the job himself this time to pick up some money for debts.

Bertone was motivated to make some drug deals and Rosa was happy to bring him into the ring. That was likely a mistake. Bertone proceed to set up his own scams. Bertone reportedly cheated George "Sonny" Jordan, owner of a trucking company in Duquesne in a $100,000 drug deal. He delivered Jordan sugar instead of cocaine. He then staged a robbery of the sugar and graciously offered to loan Jordan the money at a high interest rate to repay his debts on the failed deal.

Rosa had gotten wind that Bertone had a plan to cheat him as well in a $20,000 deal. Bertone disappeared in 1985 and has still not been found. He was at Jordan's truck yard the night he went missing. Rosa testified that when he arrived that he saw someone other than Bertone driving his car away. It was later found behind a hotel in Harmar Township just off the turnpike.

Porter may have ordered the hit. It was no secret that Porter was telling people that Bertone was not for long. In addition to the swindles, Bertone had argued with Geno Chiarelli. Rosa testified later that Chiarelli supplied the gun.

What Rosa knew and didn't know about Bertone is up for debate. Rosa called Bertone his friend. He may have witnessed the murder. He may have pulled the trigger himself or he may have not even been there that night. Rosa told several different stories, often bragging to fellow cons that they were sitting next to the man that knows what happened to Bertone. He even went as far to say that Bertone is buried in Level Green, a small community in Westmoreland County.

One of Rosa's stories, the one he would tell in court, would have led you to believe that Jordan may have been the one that pulled the trigger that night in Duquesne. Jordan may have either done the job as a favor to or on the orders of Porter and Chiarelli. Jordan could not defend himself against the accusations. He died in a traffic accident on a Western New York highway in 1988.

Rosa's luck ran out at the tender age of 29. He was arrested for running a large-scale cocaine ring in 1989 and sentenced to ten years in prison. He was brought down by a fellow dealer that was arrested earlier, Marvin Droznek. Droznek turned informant and tape-recorded conversations with Rosa as well as bought drugs from him as part of the sting.

Rosa was quick to make his own deal. He was the star witness in the 1990 Rico trial that secured jail time for Raucci, Porter, Chiarelli, Sosa and five others on drug trafficking charges. The Bertone murder charges had to be dropped because under cross examination, Rosa looked as guilty as those standing trial.

Rosa's sentence was reduced to four years, and he was placed in protective custody. Genovese supposedly told Sica that it wasn't his fault and that we didn't do this kind of thing in the old days. Sica passed away in 1991.

Genovese avoided prosecution, but that fateful day at the Holiday House may have weighed on his mind. His closest associates were now serving time. Several of them suspected Rosa robbed Mannarino, and Genovese probably had the opportunity to rid himself of the young and restless Rosa then. However, no one suspected that a third-generation member would be the undoing of the Pittsburgh crime family.

22 A Notorious Future

I have been asked many times to predict a future notorious event for Pittsburgh. There is still organized crime and even though there is a state-wide lottery – numbers are still a racket. It may be fitting that running numbers has been a way to prove yourself, but it also has been a life blood for neighborhoods, particular poorer ones. There is an underground that continues age old vice like gambling and prostitution. Human trafficking flows through the city as do drugs with heroin a major issue. Political corruption on local levels and white-collar crime on many levels still exists as well.

It could be the next designer drug. It could be the growing cybercrimes. Perhaps, the threat will come from the outside with a foreign power bringing down the complex financial, tech or medical industries that have replaced steel as the backbone of the area's economy.

I prefer to speculate that it could come out of one of our most respected and prestigious institutions, Carnegie Mellon University. Why did I make this choice? The University is at the forefront of many technologies, spinning out many startups in a variety of solutions and sectors. What catches my attention is their close relationship and secretive development with United States Defense Department.

One of the many high-tech labs at Carnegie Mellon University

Consider the possibility that one of these developments is used in the name of national security. Maybe used against a foreign power such as North Korea, China, or Russia. Maybe something goes wrong. That would qualify as a notorious event on an international scale that Pittsburgh would be credited with – even if they did not want that kind of credit.

The below is a work of fiction that takes place in the near future.

The Bunker at Carnegie Mellon

The Alarm on Rahul's phone was chirping it seemed inside his head. He rolled over a little too quick to turn it off, and the chirping turned to log splitting. He instinctively moved his hand to his throbbing head.

"Shit," was all he could muster. His mind was still in a champagne fog from last night's celebrations of a successful mission.

He felt at the covers beneath him, realizing this was his own bed. He had not seen it in nearly three months. Every waking and sleeping moment before the deployment was spent in the bunker with bad coffee and a cot taken on regular intervals. God, this felt good.

"Shit," came out again. This time it was the realization that he only had 20 minutes to cover the six blocks from his apartment to the middle of campus. No time for a shower, he slowly pulled himself up, trying to ignore his throbbing head.

He passed his sleeping roommate on the way to the bathroom. Rahul envied Jerry Chan for a moment. "Theoretical physicists have it easy," he thought as he passed him. "But I have far more lucrative job prospects."

In the bathroom, he splashed cold water onto his face in an effort to reverse the damage of last night. A quick wipe off and some deodorant before pulling on a pair of nearly clean jeans and a Carnegie Mellon hoodie.

He was out the door and racing with eleven minutes left to make it. He had to make it, or he would face incessant ribbing for not being able to hold his alcohol. The bunker was in the center of the Carnegie Mellon campus. He knew a few short cuts, but only one would bring him past the coffee cart. That was the only one worth taking.

"Please don't be a line," Rahul chanted this over and over. He rounded the corner and salvation came into sight. "No line. That's odd," he said out loud. It was followed by "Please be open," was the prayer that followed.

Slightly out of breath but pleased, Rahul's curiosity starts the conversation with Liz the Barista. "Where is everybody?" As Liz is about to provide her theories on the topic, Rahul catches a glimpse of the clock behind her left shoulder.

"Shit!" Rahul interjected.

"Excuse me?" Liz startled.

"Sorry, sorry. Very late. Need a double shot Caffe Americano."

Hot coffee in hand, Rahul gingerly sprinted the last few blocks of campus to the nondescript black façade building that acted as cover for the bunker. He entered the doors and went to Office 106 in the back. He keyed himself in and passed the three or so empty cubicles that were set dressing.

In the rear of the small office was a panel. Raul scanned his retina and placed his hand on the fingerprint scanner. The panel slid back, revealing an elevator. He pressed down. He was only 2 minutes late and took the time to slow his breathing and put on his best nonchalant look.

When the door slid open, it was eerily quiet. Gone was the frivolity of the previous night. The team had celebrated years of research into their nano bloom technology. It culminated in the first release last night over an area of dragon. The nano technology would have felt like a droplet of rain as it floated to the ground.

The tiny droplets were formulated to mix with the environment. If they landed in the right sort of mix, that would bloom into a specialized chemical weapon capable of wiping out the targeted population silent and untraceable. If they met with an environment that they were not programmed for, they would simply deactivate harmlessly.

It was serious technology funded into the hundreds of millions of dollars by the defense department. It was the most precise first strike weapon and it was now successfully deployed on a weapons complex in China.

Rahul and his teammates did not celebrate the destruction that weapon had caused last night. They celebrated years of hard work with graduate assistant pay. The good times were ahead. They could write their own ticket and would have funders lining up to throw dollars at the commercial applications that would evolve from the lethal application.

Rahul believed he was doing good for his adopted country. His family had emigrated for higher paying jobs when he was 12. His education was a product of this better life, and he was every bit if not more patriotic than the native son born to Pittsburgh.

His growing smile about the dream to come was quickly interrupted as he turned the corner and opened the door to the control room. Instead, the hair on his back stood up. Something was wrong, very wrong.

His first indication was there should have been two in the room. His second indicator was that one that was supposed to be in the room was slumped over the workstation not moving. That person was Sara Fine, Rahul's fellow research assistant.

"Sara?" Rahul tentatively questioned the motionless body. He ventured closely and noticed that blood was pooling on the floor beneath her. Rahul should have panicked, but his research nature pushed him closer. It appeared that Sara had been shot in the back of the head. He felt for a pulse that he deep down he knew would not be there.

She was dead. Rahul suppressed a scream, and it came out as a whimper. He wanted to run. Get as far away from that place as possible. Then another though crossed his mind. Where was Dr. David Dillinger? He was on duty as the project lead with Sara. Rahul started to search for him and then stopped.

"Wait - Alice was to replace him on duty, and she would have been early, unlike Rahul," thought Rahul. Where was Alice then? He frantically ran from the room yelling, "Alice!" There was no sign of anyone else and no answer to his frantic calls.

Rahul was alone. Sara was dead. David and Alice were missing. He needed to call the police. He went into one of the empty offices and picked up the receiver. No, flashed in his head. This was a security situation. He needed to call the contact at Defense. The secure phone was in the control room.

Rahul forced himself back into the room. It wasn't quiet anymore. There was an incessant beeping coming from the China theater monitors. It was a warning light. Things were about to get worse for Rahul. The trouble was not contained to just the Pittsburgh lab.

Rahul snatched the receiver for the secure phone. It dialed automatically. "O'Leary," was the gruff response on the other end. "The lantern's been knocked over," Rahul read back the security response.

"Location?"

"Tartan Primary Bunker. Project Silent Dragon," replied Rahul, keeping his voice steady.

There was a moment of awkward silence on the other end triggered by the project name. Rahul sensed a moment of panic in the realization before the voice on the other line returned to protocol.

"Your name?"

"Rahul Pradip, Graduate Research Assistant. Security clearance 2471." Rahul offered.

"Who else is in the room?"

With this question, Rahul could not help the catch in his voice, "No one else is here. One person is dead. Two others are missing. And…

The voice on the other line interrupted him, "Wait there. Do not touch anything. A security team has been dispatched and will be there within 20 minutes. Understand?"

"But" Rahul tried to continue.

"But nothing! Wait there for the security team!" The voice on the other line commanded before abruptly ending the call.

Twenty minutes is a short time. That is unless you are standing in a control room with a dead friend and a warning light beeping. With your mind racing, that amount a time can seem like a lifetime, especially when you don't know what was going to come bursting through the door.

Rahul tried to suppress the thoughts of what might come next and the imminent harm that he might now be facing. He noticed his coffee sitting on the console where he left it.

He took a sip. It was lukewarm, but nothing ever tasted so good.

He decided he needed to fully assess the situation, so he was prepared to answer the questions. First thing first, what is this warning light. He moved over to the China monitoring area. Just last night, the four were together as the nano blooms were dropped over Gansu province in China.

China was chosen because the Defense Department knew that any event would be suppressed by the government. It would be like a new disease and China would work to contain it without informing anyone, including their own citizens and certainly not the World Health Organization.

Gansu is landlocked deep into the center part of the country. It is home to mines and very rocky. It also hides a secret advanced weapons facility. One that was deemed as a significant threat to the United States.

The country's top defense minds had spent decades trying to devise a plan to access and destroy it. There simply was no way to access it with conventional warfare. The area was isolated and well protected. Then nano technology came along.

The nano bloom could be released from a high-altitude drone. By the time China responded, the package would be delivered and wouldn't be able to be detected by any current technology. Everything would look harmless. That is until the nano bloom found its environmental signature.

In this case, it was limestone. Sensing this it would activate, blooming in two stages. In the first stage, it would emit an EMF signal that would take all electronics including the advanced weaponry.

The second stage was designed to cripple the program. The nano bloom changed to a deadly gas, killing any humans in the designated area, and poisoning it for decades to keep everyone away.

If the wind carried the nano bloom to the surrounding irrigated plains or as far as the Yellow River, it would not see its environmental signature and would not activate, lying dormant and undetected until it would be washed away.

When Rahul looked at the monitor, he saw the red area signifying the nano bloom over the target as expected. His draw dropped as he saw red bursts spreading from the location away from the target and into the surrounding areas. Areas populated by farmers, fisherman, and merchants. Collateral damage would be ordinary Chinese citizens men, women and children.

"This can't be happening," exclaimed Rahul.

The nano bloom should have shut itself down. Instead, it seems to have mutated accepting additional environmental signatures to multiply and spread. Rahul had no idea how this could have happened nor if it would stop on its own. He did know this - it could not be stopped from here. Nano blooms were engineered without limited broadcast abilities to prevent tracing. That might have been a fatal flaw.

Before Rahul could ponder this further. He heard from the hallway outside, the word "Clear" repeated several times. The door to the control room burst open and several automatic weapons were pointed at him.

"Hands up," the lead gun commanded. "On your knees, face me!"

Rahul did as commanded. He was patted down aggressively, and plastic hand ties were fastened around his hands.

"Who are you," asked the lead gun.

"Rahul, please, I made the call."

Another two guns entered the control room. "The place is clean," they reported.

The lead gun ignored Rahul. He was connected by headset to someone in another location. "Confirmed. Subject is in custody. Confirmed one casualty on site. Confirmed no sign of forced entry. No other suspects."

"Put him on," said the voice. The lead gun pulled Rahul roughly from his knees, handing him the headset.

"Rahul, this does not look good. Why don't you tell me what is going on," said the voice.

"Who is this?" Rahul answered shakily.

"I am in charge of Project Dragon for our government, that is all you need to know," answered the voice. "But if helps call me Sam."

"How do I know you are in charge," answered Rahul.

"Because I ordered the Gansu drop and I can have the man standing next to you shoot you and not lose any sleep," explained the voice.

"Ok. Ok. I came in for monitoring shift and found Sara dead. There was no one else here," answered Rahul.

"And who was on duty with Ms. Fine," asked the voice.

"Dr. Dillinger," said Rahul. "Dr. Harbinger should have replaced him."

"Neither were there then. How do you know Harbinger replaced Dillinger," said the voice.

"Because I was a few minutes late," said Rahul.

"I see, so you have no idea what happened, where the others are or why the nano bloom is spreading further into China," asked the voice.

"No. You have to believe me."

"Rahul, I don't know what to believe. I do know this - you are going to cooperate completely. Do you understand what I mean by that," commanded the voice.

"I think so, but there are four more scheduled drops. We need to. We must stop them," said Rahul with concern.

"I will worry about the drops. You will help these men disassemble the lab quickly. Pack up the control room equipment, all the research files, and the nano printer and materials. Got it," asked the voice.

"Yes."

"Good. Get moving. We will talk later when you are in a safe location. Follow the instructions of the man in the headset. You can call him Greg. Give the headset back to him," said the voice.

Rahul did as he was instructed. The man replaced the headset to his ear. "Yes, sir?"

"Check in with me when you get him to the safe house. He is to be kept under guard. No communication. Burn the lab."

"Yes sir."

Three hours later, Rahul helped one of the security team roll the last of the equipment into a moving van with markings Uncle Sam and Sons Moving and Storage. The tagline read, "Uncle Sam Has You Covered."

Rahul's clothes were covered and sweat and though he was exhausted, everything still seemed unreal as he climbed into the back of the second black SUV. As the convoy rolled past the closed-up coffee cart, he could not help but wonder if that was his last good coffee for the foreseeable future.

When the convoy turned the corner onto Forbes Avenue, Raul could see smoke rising to the sky from the direction of the bunker. He had spent the good part of five years in that place, it was like using a home. He didn't even know if they had removed poor Sara's body. In fact, he didn't know much of anything.

"This is not the way I envisioned moving up into a government position," he mumbled under his breath as emergency sirens blared in the passing distance.

To Be Continued...

Afterword

I hope you enjoyed reading this small excerpt of Pittsburgh's notorious stories. There are more that could not fit in this book – many more. Pittsburgh is more than 250 years old as a city. And the area is far older. With that many years, of course, there will be stories and legends.

Couple that with the importance as an industrial center, the gateway of its three rivers, and the diversity of peoples that have called it home and staked their lives in it. Titans built fortunes on the back of its people and resources, many without abandon or morals.

Hopes have been crushed. Fortunes gained. Lives celebrated while others were snuffed out too soon. In the shadows, where corners are cut, and ambition unchecked – that is where the notorious stories lived.

Follow those leads through obstacles and dead ends, and you will find them. Characters out of a novel and stories that read like a screenplay. I will be happy to continue to serve as your guide.

Thank you to everyone that has come on a tour for this book. You served as this book's first test audiences and your feedback has been key to shaping the stories. Your tidbits of I heard this or remember this opened additional avenues and brought personality to the writing.

Thank you to the journalists that came before me. One of the most valuable assets that we have in this digital age is the opportunity to look back on the facts as they were reported at the time by talented investigators and writers.

Thank you also to the keepers of history. This is a diverse group including established organizations like Pittsburgh History and Landmarks that documented buildings as they were and as they became. This group also includes the passionate historians and storytellers toiling away in love at small historical organizations or just in their basement. I humbly hope to be recognized as one of these folks.

Thank you to The Pittsburgh Foundation that inadvertently set me on this adventure. Also, to Pittsburgh Community Television and Doors Open Pittsburgh which continued to challenge me to come up with the next story.

Lastly, thank you to the people of Pittsburgh past, present and future. You have made this such an interesting place and I look forward to the good and the notorious stories of the future.

Stay curious!

The Tour Loops

Taking Liberty: Pittsburgh's Red-Light Tour

Start at Market Square

25 Market Square – The Mayan Health Club. Nick DeLucia used this location for his office after the Gemini was bombed. On a hot August night, he bounded down the stairs shooting guns into the late-night air.

139 7th Street – Former Tambellini's Restaurant now Proper Brick Oven & Tap Room. George Lee ate dinner here the night he was murdered.

Alley behind former Tambellini's (Walk up Penn Avenue past 707/708 and turn left down alley to parking lot). Two professional gunmen shot and killed George Lee as he was getting into his car.

966 Liberty Avenue – Former site of The Stage now the August Wilson Center. Mel Cummings ran the Stage, a strip club for George Lee until Nick DeLucia muscled him out.

943 Liberty Avenue – Former Aardvark Massage Parlor now Arcade Comedy Theater. Until Arcade moved in, you could still see the faded-out letters on the window advertising this location as a massage parlor.

823 Penn Avenue – Former Taurean Massage Parlor now Pizza Parma. The Taurean was the headquarters for Dante "Tex" Gill. It was originally a three-story building but was firebombed in 1980.

807 Liberty Avenue – Formerly the Art Cinema now Pittsburgh Cultural Trust event center. This was the first theater to start showing X-rated films. The Harris Theater next door also was an X-rated movie theater.

801 Liberty Avenue – Formerly the Roman V Massage Parlor now Crazy Mocha. After the theaters on the block went red-light, this space opened to serve the same clientele.

641 Liberty Avenue – Former location of the Gemini Massage Parlor now EQT Plaza. The Gemini was the flagship massage parlor for George Lee and Nick DeLucia after him. It was the site of the infamous Christmas Bombing.

Return to Market Square.

Notorious Pittsburgh Tour

Start at PPG Place.

125 Fourth Avenue – Former Showboat Club now part of PPG Place. There have been many infamous night club establishments in Pittsburgh, but the Showboat stood out. The Showboat belonged to the Pittsburgh family of La Cosa Nostra and one of the best ran it – Geno Chiarelli.

120 Boulevard of the Allies – National Bioskills Laboratory building. During Prohibition, illegal booze was run from the river through tunnels to the basement.

212 Boulevard of the Allies – Recently demolished. This former building was home to the longest serving brothel in Pittsburgh.

300-398 Smithfield Street – Oxford Centre Parking Garage. Food critic Mike Kalina had an unusual last meal here.

503 Court Place –This was the former location of the Court Bar, owned by George Lee and Anthony Lagatutta. It was popular with lawyers, judges, politicians, prostitutes and organized crime.

520 Third Avenue – Chinatown Inn. The China Town Inn is the last remaining example of Pittsburgh's former China Town which once stretched from Fourth Avenue to the Monongahela River.

440 Ross Street – Allegheny County Courthouse and former prison. In 1902, Katherine Soffel broke Charles Biddle out of prison and went on the run.

527 Fifth Avenue - John Volpe got the last shave of his life. It was Friday July 29, 1932. Volpe stopped in most days for a shave and a shoeshine and on Saturdays for a haircut at this second-floor barber shop.

436 Grant Street – Grant Street. Before this was Grant Street, it was Grant's Hill. When the hill was excavated to develop the street, a Native American burial ground was discovered. And strange skeletons of the former Allegewi tribe were found.

414 Grant Street – Mayor Caliguiri Statue. Say hi to Mayor Caliguiri in his pensive state. The Christmas Bombing was just one of the events that vexed him.

426 Fourth Avenue – Former Farmer's and Mechanics Bank now Fourth Avenue Parking Garage. Site of Pittsburgh's first bank robbery (Walk down Fourth Avenue from Grant Street and take in the historic banking district architecture.)

Return to PPG Place

Selected Bibliography

Chapter 1

Jack Grochot (1972, Nov. 29) Flaming Past Ends in 5-Year Prison Term for Arsonist. *The Pittsburgh Press*. Page 2.

William McCloskey (1976, Nov. 16) Parole Violation Jails Slay Suspect Lagattuta. *Pittsburgh Post-Gazette*. Page 13.

Paul Maryniak (1976, Aug. 1976) Arson Probed in Penn Ave. Fire. *The Pittsburgh Press*. Page 1.

No Author (1976, Dec. 17) Executive Lounge Agrees to Vacate, Pay Rent Due. *Pittsburgh Post-Gazette*. Page 32.

Roy McHugh (1977, March 3) Fatal Barroom Brawl Replayed in Court. *The Pittsburgh Press*. Page 2.

Edward Jensen (1976, Dec. 1) Club Fine Tied to Lagatutta Visits. *Pittsburgh Post-Gazette*. Page 37.

Doug Harbrecht (1977, March 5) Ninny Hit Floor, Too, Trial Told. *The Pittsburgh Press*. Page 2.

Chapter 2

Special Telegram (1911, Mar. 20) Crowd Chases Picture Man Out of Town. *The Pittsburgh Post-Gazette*. Page 2.

Friday Morning Post (1902, Jan. 31) The Prison Drama *Pittsburgh Daily Post*. Page 6.

Editorial Section (1903, Jan. 25) Escape of Notorious Biddle Brothers Took Place Just a Year Ago *The Pittsburgh Press*. Page 9.

Sunday Press (1901, Jun. 13) Truth in Tales of Three Thieves *The Pittsburgh Press*. Page 1.

Ray Sprigle (1949, May 1) My Biggest Stories. *The Pittsburgh Post-Gazette*. Page 27.

Chapter 3

John Dauer (1959, Jul. 27) End of the Road for Chinatown. *The Pittsburgh Post-Gazette.* Page 17.

Charles Danver (1928, Sep. 22) Vanishing Chinatown. *The Pittsburgh Post-Gazette.* Page 6.

A.P. (1927, Mar. 25) Three More Men Shot as Tong Hostilities Reopen. *The Pittsburgh Post-Gazette.* Page 1.

No Author (1928, Jan. 4) Chinatown Attends George Lee Funeral. *The Pittsburgh Post-Gazette.* Page 13.

Chapter 4

No Author (1936, Sep. 26) Battle of Grant's Hill One of World's Oddest. *The Pittsburgh Post-Gazette.* Page 38.

Alligewi Indians. https://talligewiindians.weebly.com/

Chapter 5

Jane McAnallen (2016, Jun. 29) Ghosts Haunt Downtown Pizza Place. *The Globe Online.* Page 1

Melissa McCart (2013 Dec. 6) Owner Closes PaPa J's in City. *The Pittsburgh Post-Gazette.* Page 19.

Chapter 6
No Author (1886, Jul. 29) First Bank Robbery. *The Pittsburgh Commercial Gazette.* Page 15.

Editorial (1830, Jan. 8) Remarks on the Pardon of Pluymart. *The Pittsburgh Weekly Gazette.* Page 3.

No Author (1920, Apr. 6) This Date in Pittsburgh's History. *The Pittsburgh Post-Gazette.* Page 6.

Chapter 7

Robert Baird (1989, Aug. 3) Man Gets 5 Years in Stolen Rifle Case. *The Pittsburgh Press.* Page 21.

Mike Buckso (1990, Oct. 10) Bertone Mystery Pervades Testimony in Racketeering Trial. *The Pittsburgh Post-Gazette*. Page 5.

Jack Grochot (1972, May 25) Showboat Club Receiver Named. *The Pittsburgh Press*. Page 2.

Torsten Ove (2012, Jun. 21) Obituary: Geno Chiarelli/Powerful Figure in Pittsburgh Mafia. *The Pittsburgh Post-Gazette*. Online obituary.

Chapter 8, 9 and 11

These chapters are inter-related and used the same source material.

Unidentified (1926, Sep 18) Jackie Davis Escapes While Brandon is on Vacation. *The Pittsburgh Daily Post*. Page 3.

Court Press Dept. (1934, Mar 5) Nettie Gordon's Relatives and Friends Trying to Assure Very Private Funeral. *The Pittsburgh Press*. Page 34.

Unidentified (1926, Oct 5) Trustee Clark Fails to Back Rev. Barker in 'Drive' on Vice. *The Pittsburgh Daily Post*. Page 1.

Unidentified (1926, Oct 9) Nettie Gordon Who Escaped Jury Trial, Eludes Jury Duty Too. *The Pittsburgh Post-Gazette*. Page 1.

Unidentified (1924, Jul 17) 14 Women Held, Taken in Raids. *The Pittsburgh Post-Gazette*. Page 4.

Unidentified (1926, Feb 8) Attempt to Steal Nettie Gordon's Rum Thwarted by Police. *The Pittsburgh Daily Post*. Page 1.

Unidentified (1925, May 23) Inspector Refuses to Clamp Lid on District. *The Pittsburgh Daily Post*. Page 1.

Mabel Walker Willebrandt (1929, Aug 28) Disastrous Results from Corrupted U.S. Commissioners. *The Pittsburgh Press*. Page 4.

Unidentified. (1932, Jul 30) City Pays 100 Millions to Racketeers in 5 Years as Bribes Total $10,000,000. *The Pittsburgh Press*. Page 8.

Unidentified. (1936, Dec 21) Police Start Vice Cleanup on North Side. *The Pittsburgh Press*. Page 1.

Unidentified (1933, May 8) Racket War Mapped by Pastors. *The Pittsburgh Sun-Telegraph*. Page 1.

Steve Mellon (2016, Dec 31) Pittsburgh the Dark Years. *The Pittsburgh Post-Gazette*. Online/Interactive.

Unidentified (1926, Aug 6) Writ to Deter Police Denied. *The Pittsburgh Post-Gazette*. Page 5.

Unidentified. (1932, Sep 7) Police Start Vice Cleanup on North Side. *The Pittsburgh Press*. Page 1.

Unidentified. (1930, Jan 16) Dry Law Has Cost Nation $235,000,000 in Decade. *The Pittsburgh Press*. Page 8.

Unidentified (1929, Jan 27) New Thrones in an Old Republic. *The Pittsburgh Sun-Telegraph*. Page 50.

Chapter 10

Various (1932, Jul 30) Slayers of Three Volpe Brothers Sought in Underworld Here. *The Pittsburgh Post-Gazette*. Page 1

Various (1932, Jul 30) Wives of Volpes Mourn For Dead. *The Pittsburgh Post-Gazette*. Page 1

Various (1932, Jul 30) Turtle Creek Under Volpe's Rule 14 Years. *The Pittsburgh Post-Gazette*. Page 2

Various (1932, Aug 12) Mysterious Bazzano's Life Unlike Volpe's; Greed Leads All 4 to Gangster Deaths. *The Pittsburgh Press*. Page 1

Various (1932, Jul 29) Gunmen Drop Trio in Hill District Raid. *The Pittsburgh Press*. Page 1

Various (1932, Aug 22) Triple Slaying Laid to John's Ex-Bodyguard. *The Pittsburgh Press*. Page 1

Chapters 12-18

These chapters are inter-related and used the same source material.

Selwyn Raab (1990, Nov 5) 'Limping relics' and the 'Geritol gang'. *The Pittsburgh Post-Gazette.* Page 5.

William McCloskey (1977, Mar 9) IRS to Use Secret Jury Info on Lee. *The Pittsburgh Post-Gazette.* Page 17.

Mary Stolberg (1980, Jul 7) Vice Probe Hunts Laundered Funds. *The Pittsburgh Press.* Page 4.

Randy Rieland (1977, Mar 2) Slain 'Vice King's' Attorney Puts Lee Funeral On Hold. *The Pittsburgh Press.* Page 4.

Charles Lynch (1977, Feb 25) Reputed Vice King George Lee Slain. *The Pittsburgh Post-Gazette.* Page 1.

Not Identified (1977, Dec 17) Scott Twp. Slaying, Mob Link Probed *The Pittsburgh Press.* Page 1.

Doug Harbrecht (1977, Dec 25) Massage King's Heritage Bloody, Estate Small. *The Pittsburgh Press.* Page 2.

Rich Gigler (1977, Dec 25) Fear Shuts Area Rub Parlors. *The Pittsburgh Press.* Page 2.

Mary Stolberg (1980, Nov 17) DeLucia Trial Skirts In-Depth View of Rub Racket. *The Pittsburgh Press.* Page 2.

Mary Stolberg (1980, Nov 12) Worked As DeLucia Prostitutes, 2 Testify At Tax Evasion Trial. *The Pittsburgh Press.* Page 14.

William McCloskey (1977, Mar 1) 2 Cleveland Men May Be Key to Porn Probe Here. *The Pittsburgh Post-Gazette.* Page 9.

Ann Butler (1977, Nov 27) Vice Lord's Friend Lives In Bull's-eye. *The Pittsburgh Press.* Page 1.

Edwina Rankin (1978, Feb 9) Slay Suspect Held On Weapon Count. *The Pittsburgh Press.* Page 10.

Mary Stolberg (1983, Aug 21) Poverty Plea Frees Rub Parlor Boss. *The Pittsburgh Press.* Page 8.

William Allan Jr. (1977, Dec 24) Package At Kingpin's Home A Real 'Present'. *The Pittsburgh Press*. Page 3.

Joyce Gemperlein (1978, Mar 23) Sciliano Admitted Slaying Pugh, Ex-Cellmate Claims. *The Pittsburgh Post-Gazette*. Page 1.

Geoff Brown (1978, Jan 28) Pugh's Girl Tells of 'Hit' Contract. *The Pittsburgh Press*. Page 1.

Rich Gigler (1977, Dec 24) 4 Rub Parlors Shut After Fatal Blast. *The Pittsburgh Press*. Page 1.

Connie Giel (1977, Dec 24) Hooker, Mate Pawns in War?. *The Pittsburgh Press*. Page 1.

Roy McHugh (1978, Apr 6) Informer In 'Hit" Contract Once Did Favors for DeLucia. *The Pittsburgh Press*. Page 2.

Unidentified (1984, Dec 16) Dubious man of the year. *The Pittsburgh Post-Gazette*. Page 487.

Team of Writers (1978, Jan 31) Cosa Nostra Family Linked to Rub Rackets and Gill Was Horsewoman Before Career in Sex. *The Pittsburgh Post-Gazette*. Page 1 and 4.

Torsten Ove (2003, Jan 9) Dante 'Tex' Gill obituary. *The Pittsburgh Post-Gazette*. Page 18.

Harry Tkach (1979, May 22) Gill Gives Up, Held In City Call-Girl Ring. *The Pittsburgh Post-Gazette*. Page 1.

Al Donalson (1985, Jan 3) Reputed rub parlor chief Tex Gill gets 13-year term for tax evasion. *The Pittsburgh Press*. Page 1.

Robert Baird (1978, Sep 26) 4 Plead Guilty in Violent Vice Raid. *The Pittsburgh Press*. Page 2.

Janet Williams (1987, Jun 17) 'Tex' Gill sues to get into halfway house. *The Pittsburgh Press*. Page 22.

Chapter 19

Unidentified (1978, May 28) Woman's Body Found; Vice War Tie Probed. *The Pittsburgh Press*. Page 1.

Jim Gallagher (1984, Jan 12) Victim's bother: Bargain is lenient. *The Pittsburgh Post-Gazette*. Page 102.

Paul Mayniak (1981, Nov 27) Probers Trace Jailbreak Try to Youngstown. *The Pittsburgh Press*. Page 8.

Carole Patton (1984, Jan 12) Bargain. Henkel pleads guilty, gets life term in killing. *The Pittsburgh Post-Gazette*. Page 1.

Harry Tkach (1983, Mar 24) U.S.; county courts try Richard Henkel. *The Pittsburgh Post-Gazette*. Page 3.

Carole Patton (1984, Jul 19) Richard Henkel shows police where he buried 2 associates. *The Pittsburgh Post-Gazette*. Page 1.

William Mausteller (1983, Apr 15) West Pen Standoff Continues. *The Pittsburgh Press*. Page 1.

Unidentified (1980, Nov 11) Airport hotel slay suspect only heir in will, court told. *The Pittsburgh Post-Gazette*. Page 17.

Linda S. Wilson (1981, May 1) Art Rooney was target of bomb-extort plot. *The Pittsburgh Post-Gazette*. Page 4.

Linda S. Wilson (1981, Oct 25) Airport slaying suspect is linked to bomb plot. *The Pittsburgh Post-Gazette*. Page 1.

Dan Kohut (1983, Jul 9) Says of terror at Western Penitentiary. *The Pittsburgh Post-Gazette*. Page 7.

Paul Mayniak (1980, Oct 23) Hampton Man Charged in Airport Slay 'Contract'. *The Pittsburgh Press*. Page 1.

Unidentified (1970, Feb 3) City Police, Magistrate in Clash. *The Pittsburgh Press*. Page 6.

Rich Gigler (1978, May 30) Brutal Slaying Called Message in City's Vice War. *The Pittsburgh Press*. Page 2.

Chapter 20

Michael A. Fuoco (1992, Feb 28) Kalina accepted food, other goods from restauranters. *The Pittsburgh Post-Gazette.* Page 29.

John G. Craig Jr. (1992, Feb 1) A sad, sad story. *The Pittsburgh Post-Gazette.* Page 9.

Bob Hoover (1991, Dec 11) Cookbook with a Pittsburgh Flavor. *The Pittsburgh Post-Gazette.* Page 18.

Marylynne Pitz (1992, Feb 1) Food critic recalled as talented, driven. *The Pittsburgh Post-Gazette.* Page 39.

Steve Creedy (1992, Feb 1) Losing reputation would've devastated Kalina, friends say. *The Pittsburgh Post-Gazette.* Page 1.

Michael A. Fuoco (1992, May 14) Grand jury to hear Kalina associate. *The Pittsburgh Post-Gazette.* Page 1.

Michael A. Fuoco (1992, Jan 30) Kalina discussed probe not long before suicide. *The Pittsburgh Post-Gazette.* Page 1.

Chapter 21 and 22

Bill Moushey (1985, Dec 23) Mafia boss sheds light on crime here. *The Pittsburgh Post-Gazette.* Page 1.

John Schmitz (1980, Jul 12) Reputed Mobster Dies Amid Mystery. *The Pittsburgh Press.* Page 3.

John Schmitz (1980, Jun 24) District Mob Figure Gets Cancer Treatment. *The Pittsburgh Press.* Page 2.

Fritz Huysman (1980, Jan 29) Mannarino Faces Grand Jury Quiz?. *The Pittsburgh Post-Gazette.* Page 10.

Susan Mannella (1980, Jul 12) Mannarino Dies at 64 of Cancer. *The Pittsburgh Post-Gazette.* Page 3.

Torsten Ove (2006, Nov 02) Government said quiet businessman was mafia boss. *The Pittsburgh Post-Gazette.* Page 20.

Mike Bucsko (1990, Sep 19) Witness says mob victimized by thieves. *The Pittsburgh Post-Gazette*. Page 4.

Torsten Ove (2000, Nov 6) Mafia has a long history here. *The Pittsburgh Post-Gazette*. Page 8.

Mike Bucsko (1990, Sep 3) Racketeering trial among largest. *The Pittsburgh Post-Gazette*. Page 7.

Mike Bucsko (1990, Sep 17) Protected witness to tell of past in city's underworld. *The Pittsburgh Post-Gazette*. Page 5.

Mike Bucsko (1990, Oct 30) 9 crime figures found guilty. *The Pittsburgh Post-Gazette*. Page 1.

Harrisburg Bureau (1970, Jul 3) Mafia Activity in Area Dates Back to 1890s. *The Pittsburgh Post-Gazette*. Page 5.

Torsten Ove (2009, Apr 19) The Life & Times Of The Last Great Pittsburgh Mobster. *The Pittsburgh Post-Gazette*. Page 63.

Mike Bucsko (1990, Oct 10) Electronic eyes watched crime family, agent says. *The Pittsburgh Post-Gazette*. Page 7.

ABOUT THE AUTHOR

Chris Whitlatch is an author, game creator, and nonprofit marketer, but he likes to be best known as a storyteller. For the past several years, he hosted two walking tours in downtown Pittsburgh, telling stories of Pittsburgh's Notorious past. He collected those stories as well as several more of his favorites into this book. He has a journalism degree from New York University but grew up in Southwestern Pennsylvania and returned to the area in 2000. Look for current and future titles at christopherwhitlatch.com.

www.ingramcontent.com/pod-product-compliance
Lightning Source LLC
Chambersburg PA
CBHW060233030426
42335CB00014B/1442